Kim's mom. Mother Lee. The OGALAG. OG stands for original or Old & Grumpy. She can't figure out why her daughter's so angry. (Like mother, like daughter!)

Bruce. Deborah's brother.
He's a meathead. But he tries.

Pat the happy little boy! He's just so happy! He wants to hang with the girls!

Mr. Sun. He's there hanging out in the sky. Sometimes Maria talks to him.

Chuy (pronounced Chew-ee).
He's a chipper chicken. Go Chuy!!!

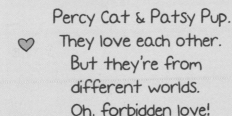

Percy Cat & Patsy Pup.
They love each other.
But they're from different worlds.
Oh, forbidden love!

boy

girl

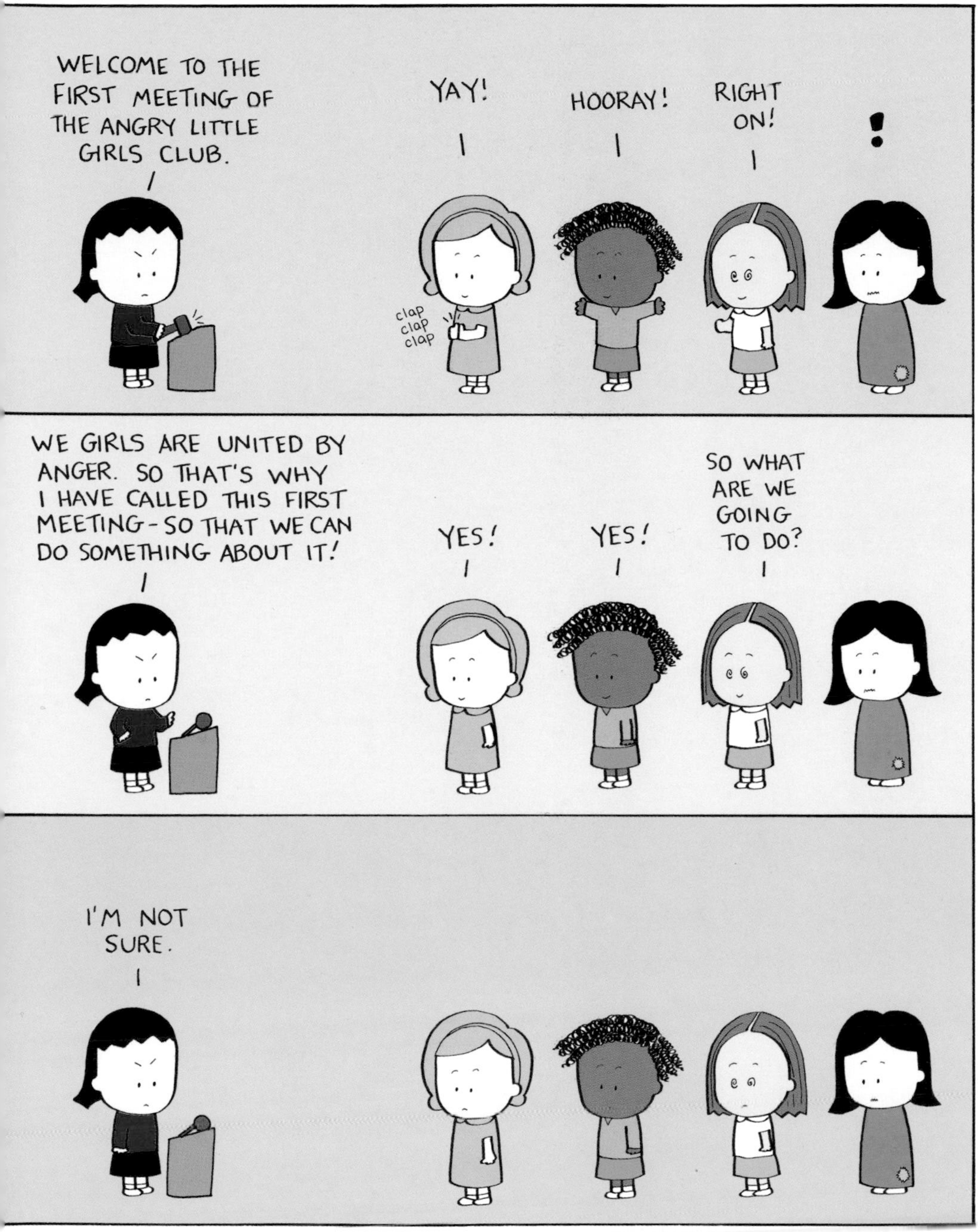
WELCOME TO THE FIRST MEETING OF THE ANGRY LITTLE GIRLS CLUB.
YAY!
clap clap clap
HOORAY!
RIGHT ON!
!
WE GIRLS ARE UNITED BY ANGER. SO THAT'S WHY I HAVE CALLED THIS FIRST MEETING - SO THAT WE CAN DO SOMETHING ABOUT IT!
YES!
YES!
SO WHAT ARE WE GOING TO DO?
I'M NOT SURE.

ANGRY
LITTLE GIRLS

by Lela Lee

Harry N. Abrams, Inc., Publishers

Special thanks to:
my keen and enthusiastic editor Linas Alsenas and the whole team at Harry N. Abrams, Inc.;
my lawyer David Rosenbaum for his sage legal advice;
my legal counsel of Amy, Jeff and Jonathan at KMOB who do stuff that confuses me;
my friend Andy who took me to the animation festival that made me mad;
my generous sister Linda who loaned me money when I was too broke to make my first
batch of T-shirts;
my wonderful husband Ken who is too great for words.

And last but most important,
the faithful readers who have stuck by me for so long...I'm finally published!

Designed by Vivian Cheng
Production Manager: Jonathan Lopes

Library of Congress Control Number: 2004109864

Text and illustrations copyright © 2005 Lela Lee

Harry N. Abrams, Inc.
100 Fifth Avenue
New York, NY 10011
www.abramsbooks.com

Abrams is a subsidiary of

LA MARTINIÈRE

FOR MY GRANDMA

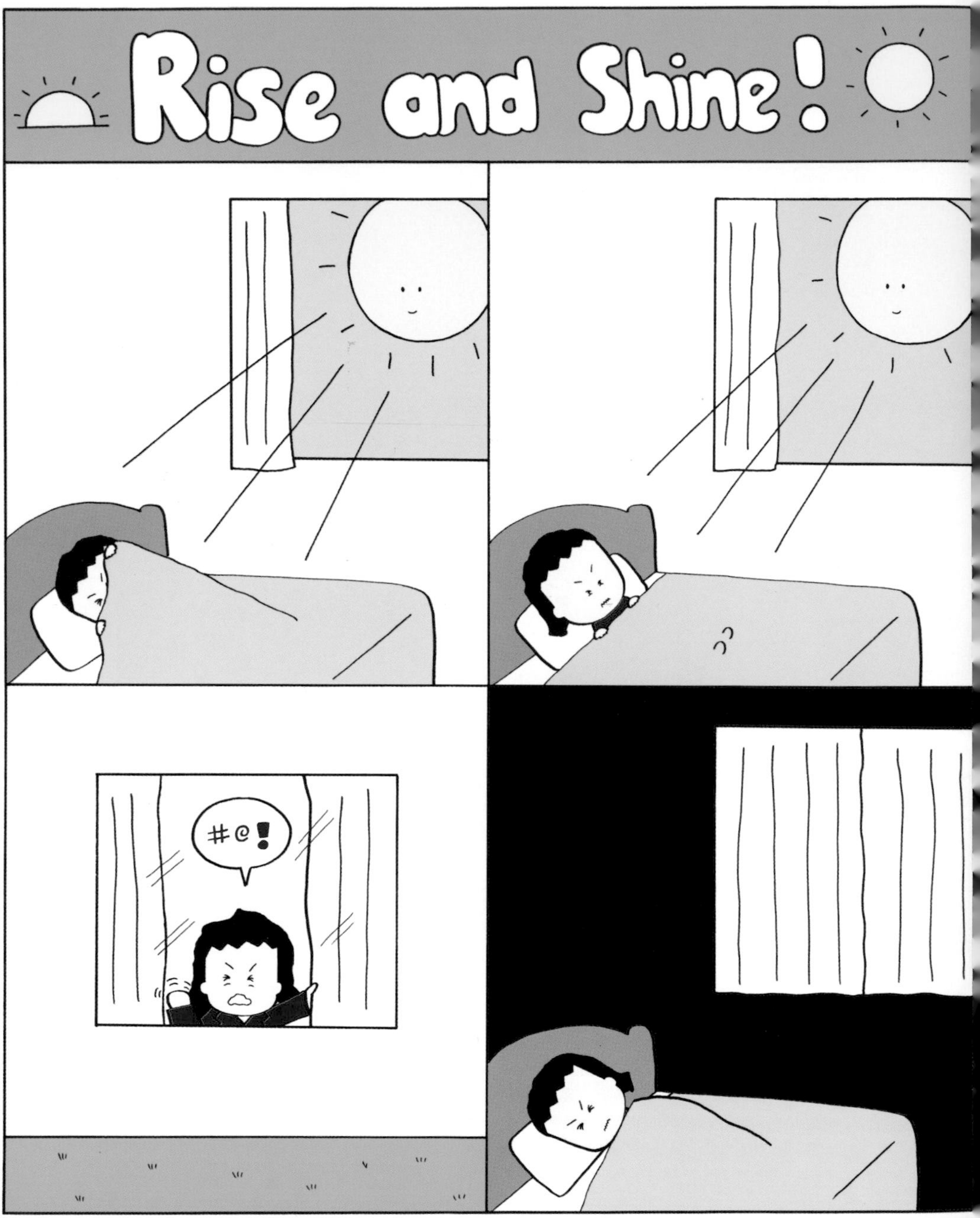
Rise and Shine!
#@!

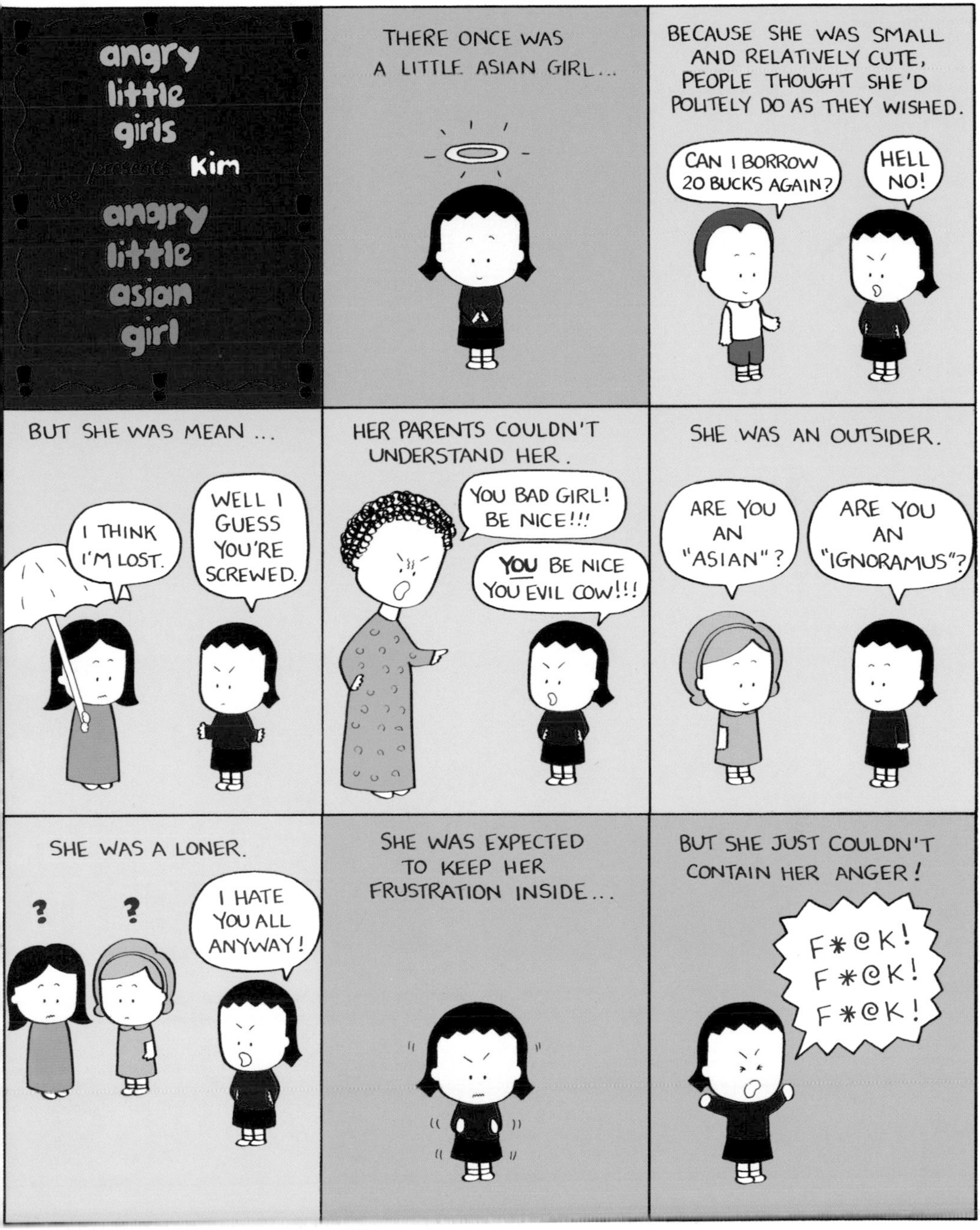
angry little girls presents kim the angry little asian girl
THERE ONCE WAS A LITTLE ASIAN GIRL...
BECAUSE SHE WAS SMALL AND RELATIVELY CUTE, PEOPLE THOUGHT SHE'D POLITELY DO AS THEY WISHED.
CAN I BORROW 20 BUCKS AGAIN?
HELL NO!
BUT SHE WAS MEAN...
I THINK I'M LOST.
WELL I GUESS YOU'RE SCREWED.
HER PARENTS COULDN'T UNDERSTAND HER.
YOU BAD GIRL! BE NICE!!!
YOU BE NICE YOU EVIL COW!!!
SHE WAS AN OUTSIDER.
ARE YOU AN "ASIAN"?
ARE YOU AN "IGNORAMUS"?
SHE WAS A LONER.
?
?
I HATE YOU ALL ANYWAY!
SHE WAS EXPECTED TO KEEP HER FRUSTRATION INSIDE...
BUT SHE JUST COULDN'T CONTAIN HER ANGER!
F*@K! F*@K! F*@K!

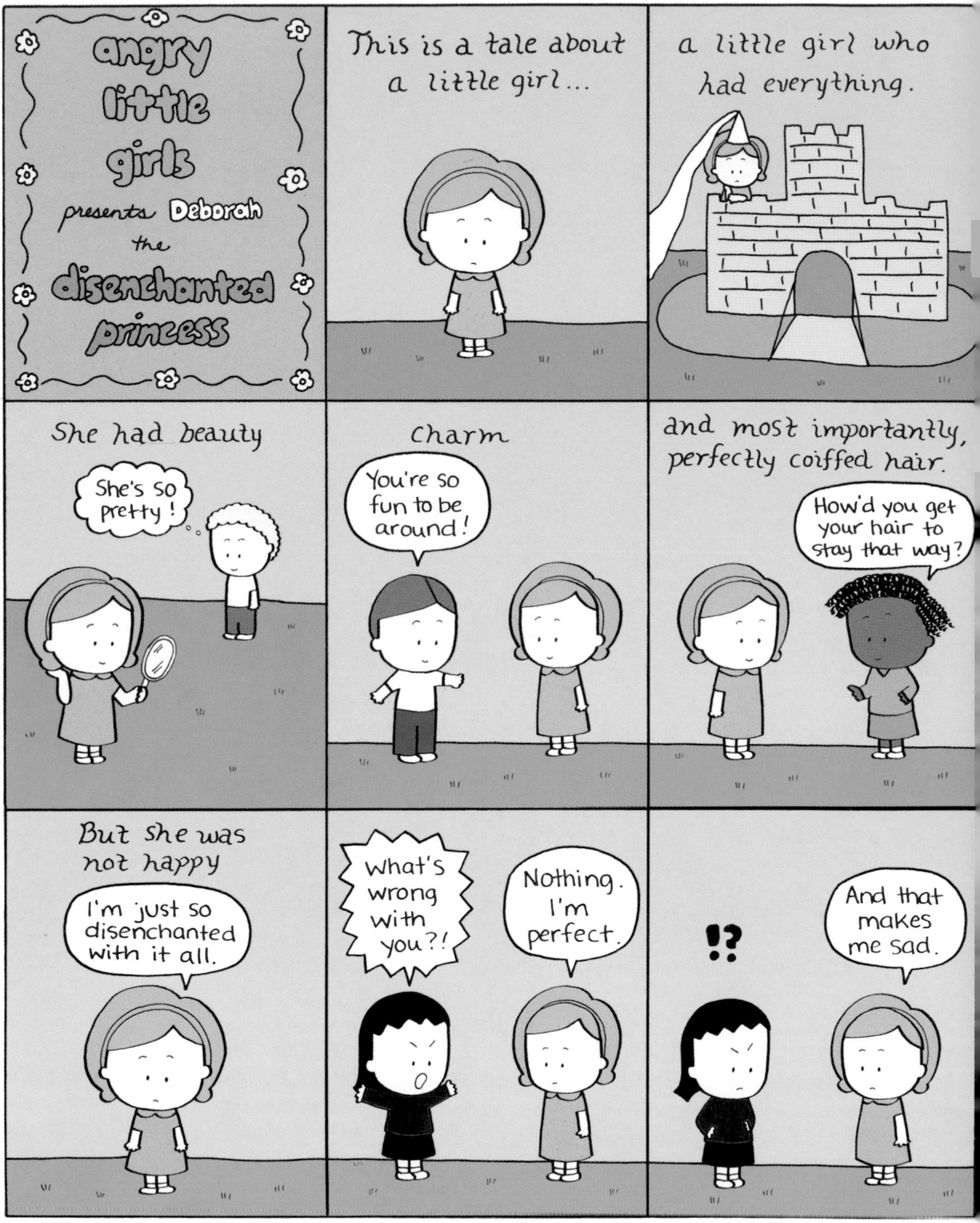
angry little girls
presents Deborah the disenchanted princess
This is a tale about a little girl...
a little girl who had everything.
She had beauty
She's so pretty!
Charm
You're so fun to be around!
and most importantly, perfectly coiffed hair.
How'd you get your hair to stay that way?
But she was not happy
I'm just so disenchanted with it all.
What's wrong with you?!
Nothing. I'm perfect.
!?
And that makes me sad.

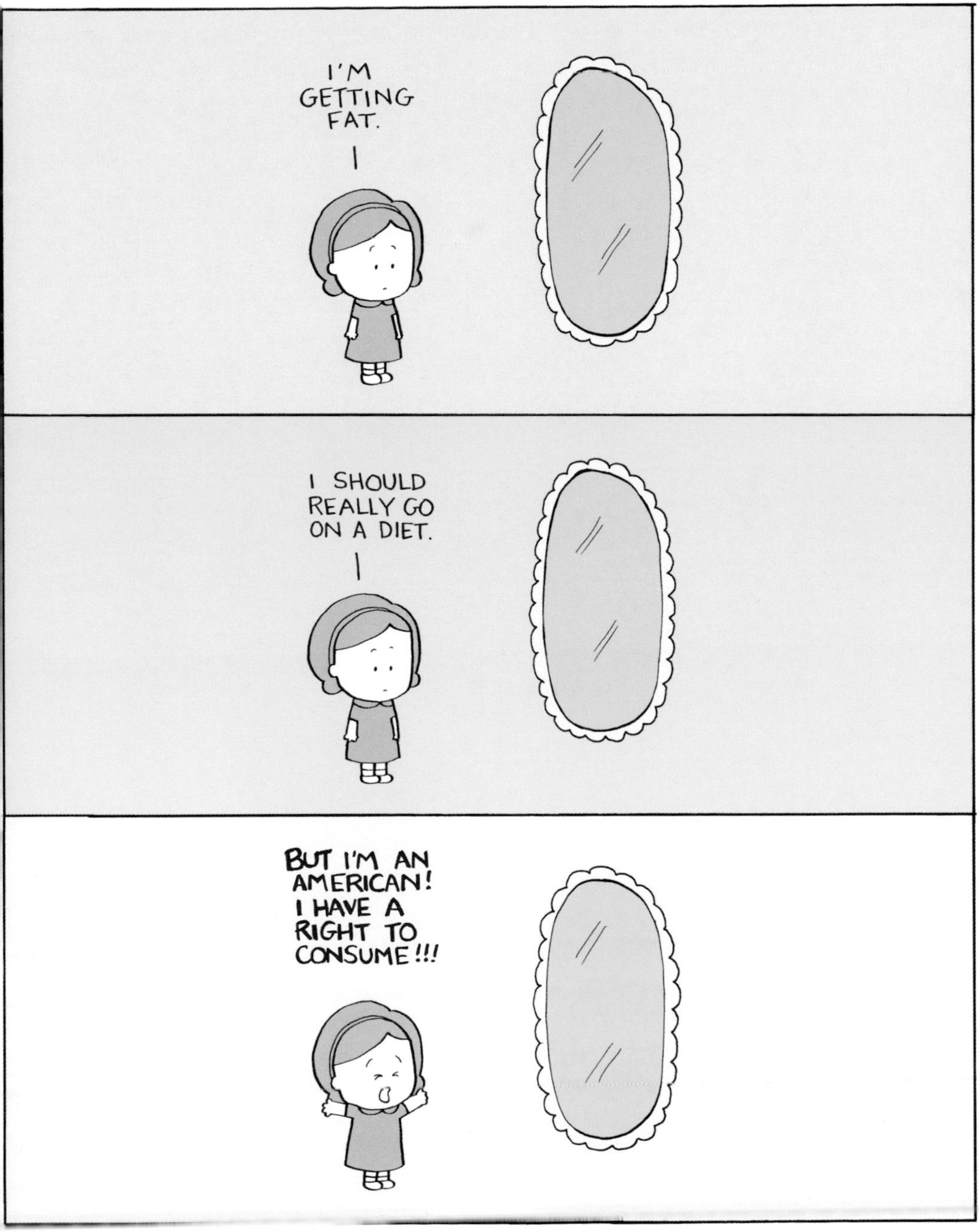
I'M GETTING FAT.
I SHOULD REALLY GO ON A DIET.
BUT I'M AN AMERICAN! I HAVE A RIGHT TO CONSUME!!!

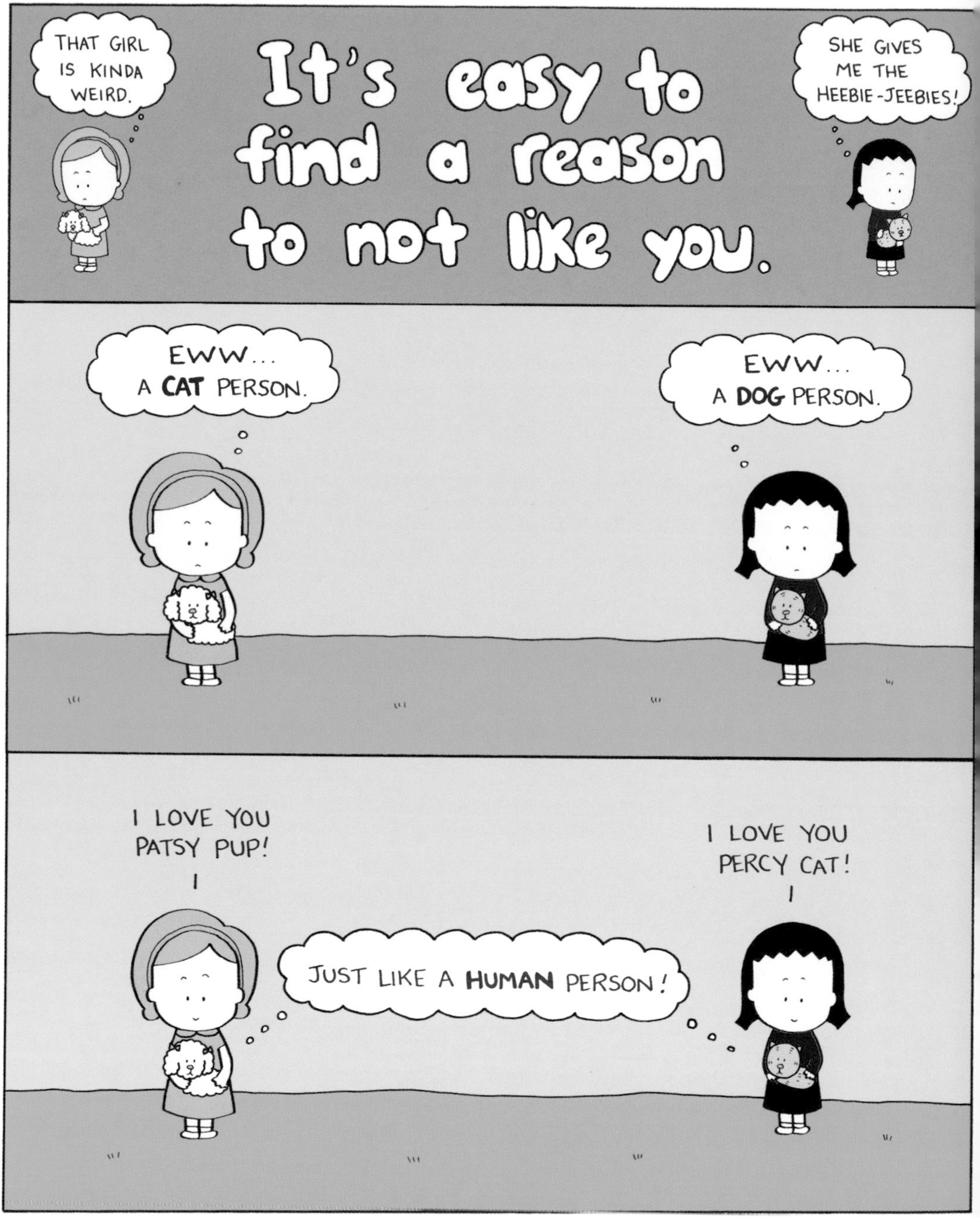
THAT GIRL IS KINDA WEIRD.
It's easy to find a reason to not like you.
SHE GIVES ME THE HEEBIE-JEEBIES!
EWW... A CAT PERSON.
EWW... A DOG PERSON.
I LOVE YOU PATSY PUP!
I LOVE YOU PERCY CAT!
JUST LIKE A HUMAN PERSON!

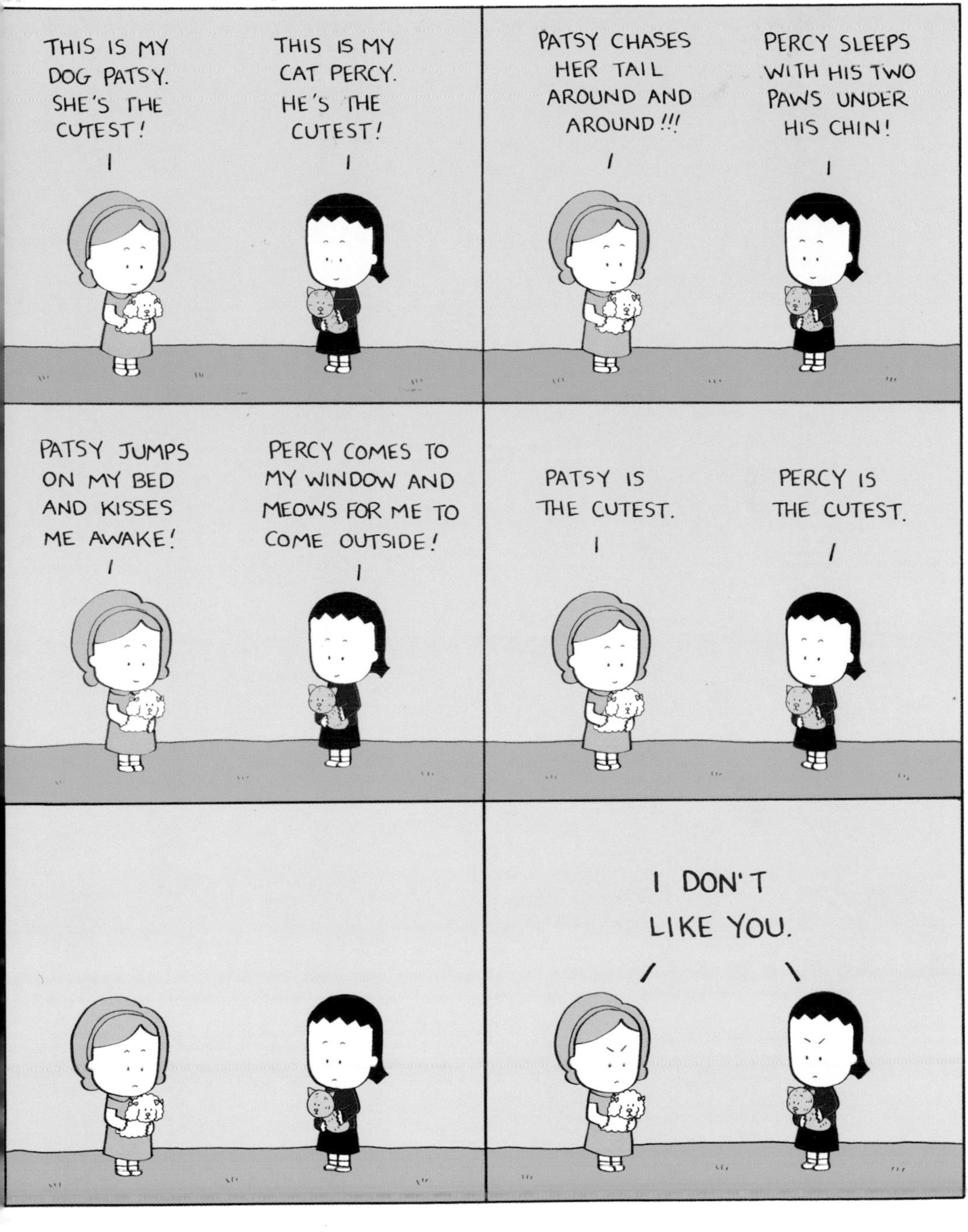
THIS IS MY DOG PATSY. SHE'S THE CUTEST!
THIS IS MY CAT PERCY. HE'S THE CUTEST!
PATSY CHASES HER TAIL AROUND AND AROUND!!!
PERCY SLEEPS WITH HIS TWO PAWS UNDER HIS CHIN!
PATSY JUMPS ON MY BED AND KISSES ME AWAKE!
PERCY COMES TO MY WINDOW AND MEOWS FOR ME TO COME OUTSIDE!
PATSY IS THE CUTEST.
PERCY IS THE CUTEST.
I DON'T LIKE YOU.

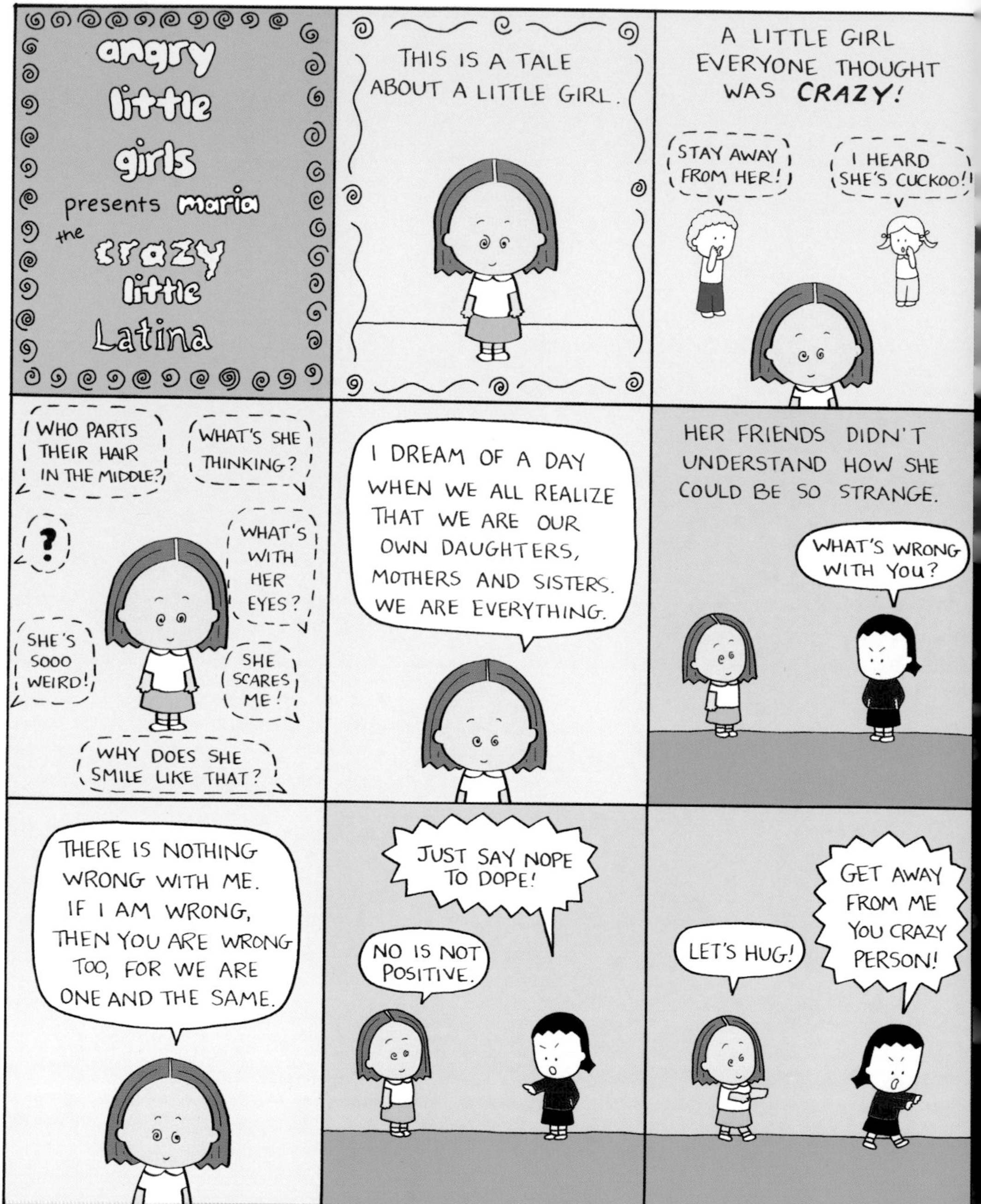
angry little girls presents maria the crazy little Latina
THIS IS A TALE ABOUT A LITTLE GIRL.
A LITTLE GIRL EVERYONE THOUGHT WAS CRAZY!
STAY AWAY FROM HER!
I HEARD SHE'S CUCKOO!
WHO PARTS THEIR HAIR IN THE MIDDLE?
WHAT'S SHE THINKING?
?
WHAT'S WITH HER EYES?
SHE'S SOOO WEIRD!
SHE SCARES ME!
WHY DOES SHE SMILE LIKE THAT?
I DREAM OF A DAY WHEN WE ALL REALIZE THAT WE ARE OUR OWN DAUGHTERS, MOTHERS AND SISTERS. WE ARE EVERYTHING.
HER FRIENDS DIDN'T UNDERSTAND HOW SHE COULD BE SO STRANGE.
WHAT'S WRONG WITH YOU?
THERE IS NOTHING WRONG WITH ME. IF I AM WRONG, THEN YOU ARE WRONG TOO, FOR WE ARE ONE AND THE SAME.
JUST SAY NOPE TO DOPE!
NO IS NOT POSITIVE.
LET'S HUG!
GET AWAY FROM ME YOU CRAZY PERSON!

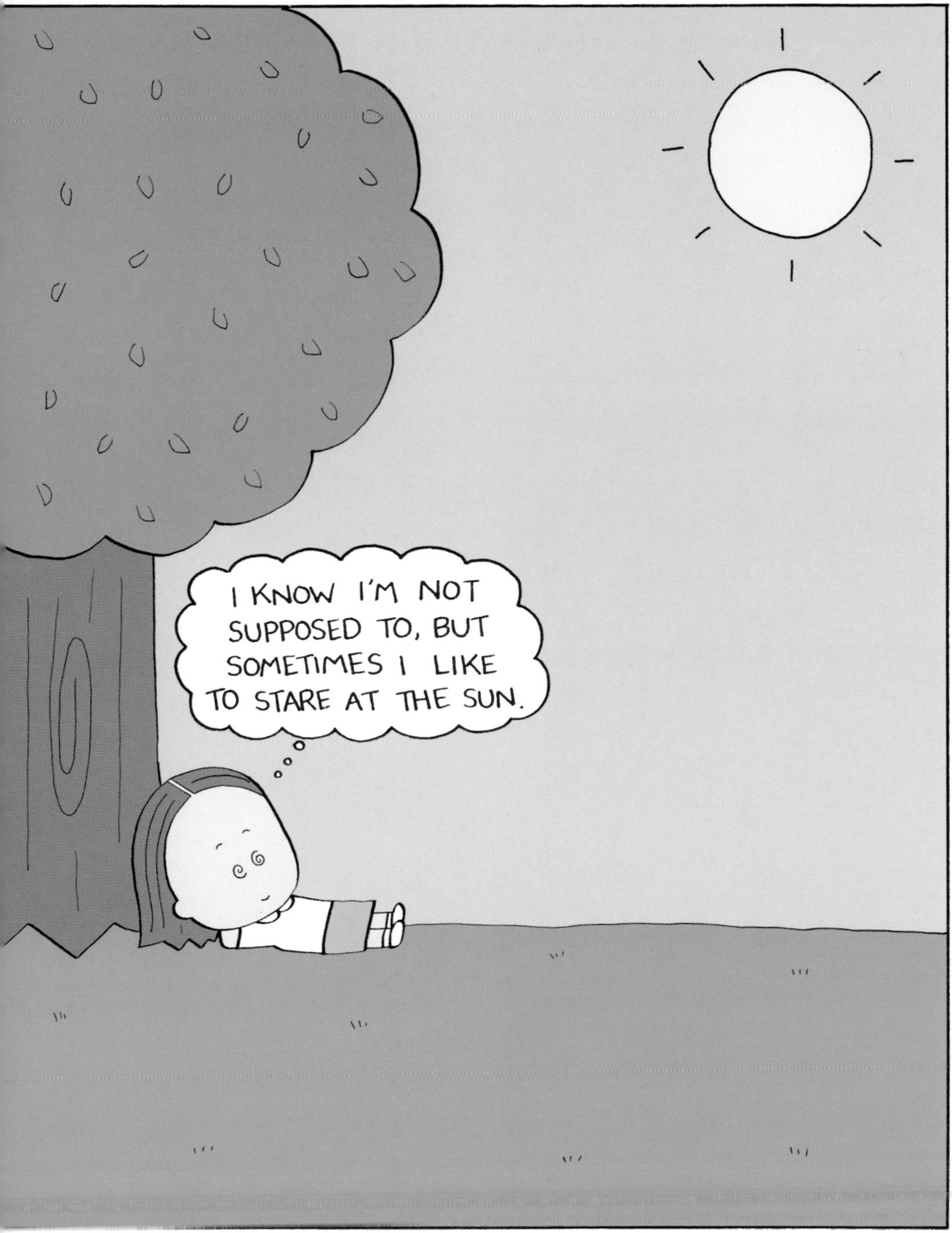
I KNOW I'M NOT SUPPOSED TO, BUT SOMETIMES I LIKE TO STARE AT THE SUN.

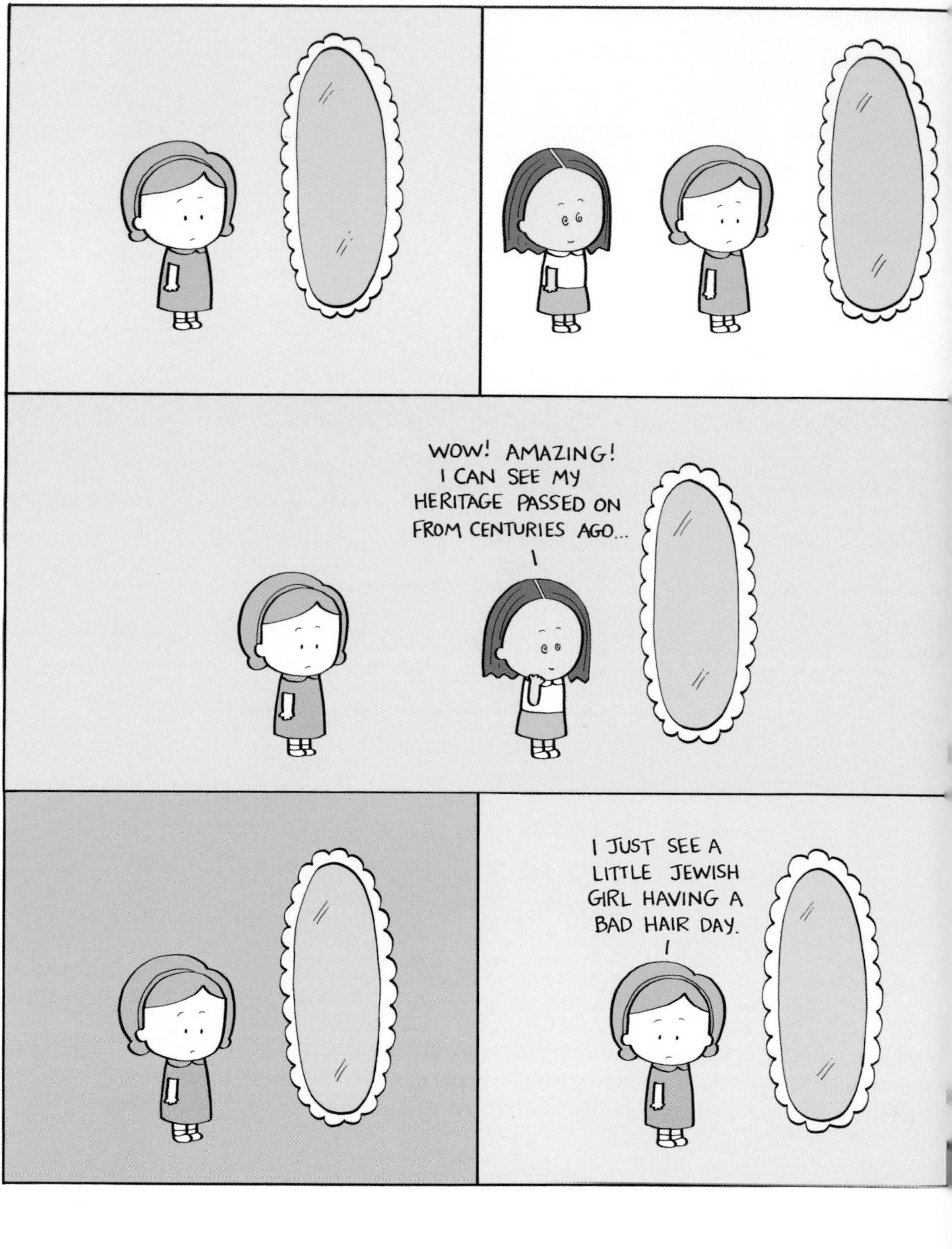
WOW! AMAZING! I CAN SEE MY HERITAGE PASSED ON FROM CENTURIES AGO...
I JUST SEE A LITTLE JEWISH GIRL HAVING A BAD HAIR DAY.

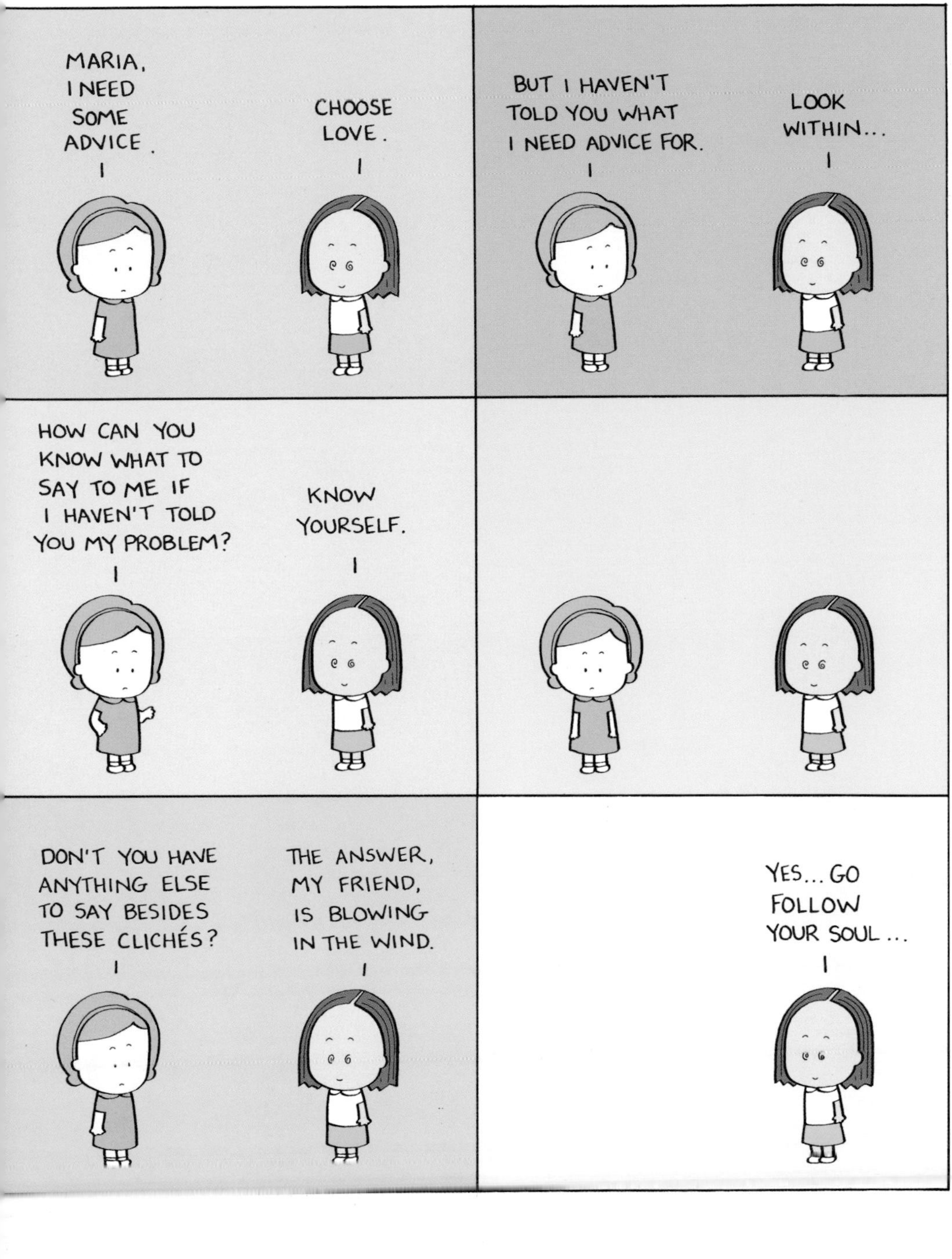
MARIA, I NEED SOME ADVICE.
CHOOSE LOVE.
BUT I HAVEN'T TOLD YOU WHAT I NEED ADVICE FOR.
LOOK WITHIN...
HOW CAN YOU KNOW WHAT TO SAY TO ME IF I HAVEN'T TOLD YOU MY PROBLEM?
KNOW YOURSELF.
DON'T YOU HAVE ANYTHING ELSE TO SAY BESIDES THESE CLICHÉS?
THE ANSWER, MY FRIEND, IS BLOWING IN THE WIND.
YES... GO FOLLOW YOUR SOUL...

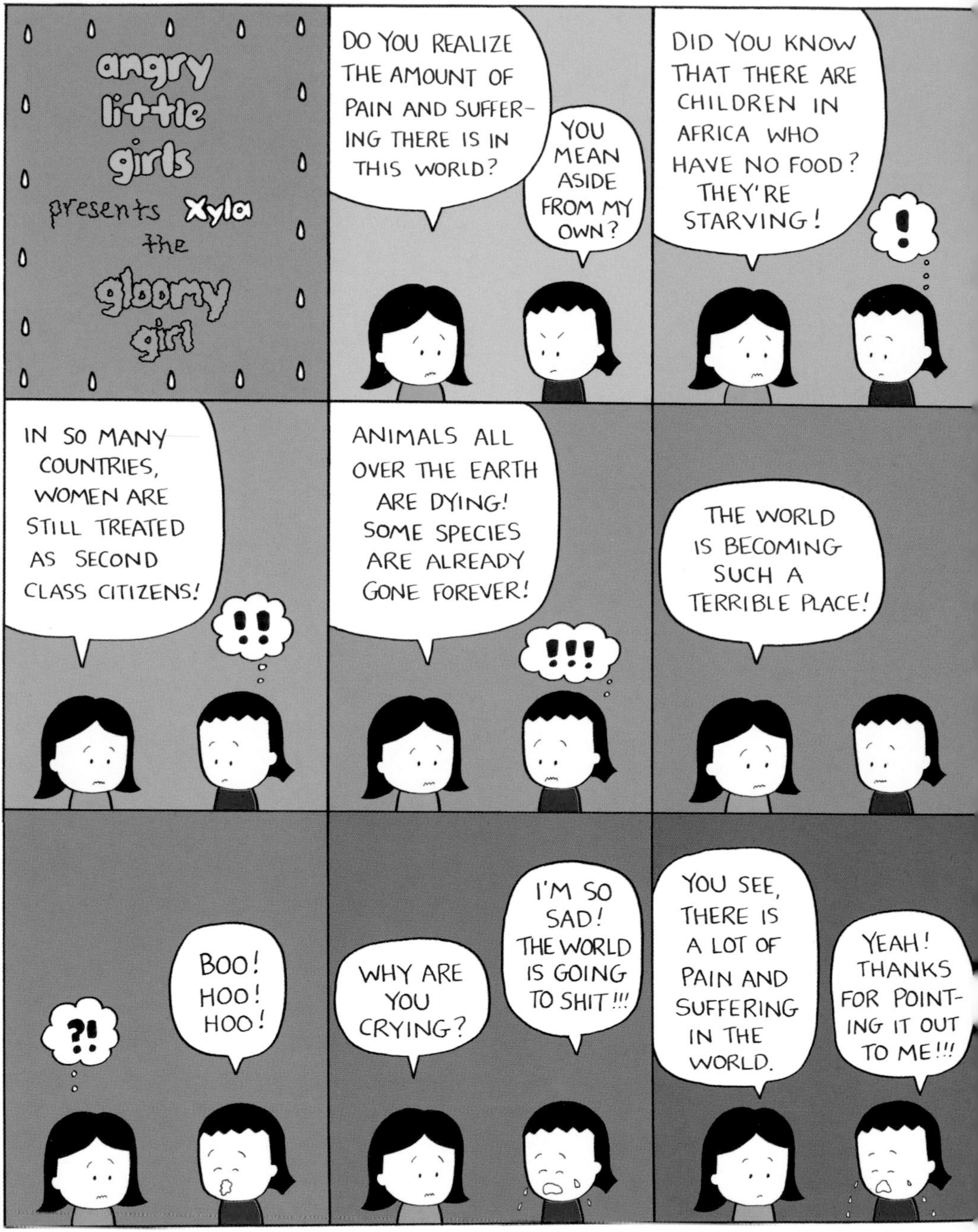
angry little girls presents Xyla the gloomy girl
DO YOU REALIZE THE AMOUNT OF PAIN AND SUFFERING THERE IS IN THIS WORLD?
YOU MEAN ASIDE FROM MY OWN?
DID YOU KNOW THAT THERE ARE CHILDREN IN AFRICA WHO HAVE NO FOOD? THEY'RE STARVING!
!
IN SO MANY COUNTRIES, WOMEN ARE STILL TREATED AS SECOND CLASS CITIZENS!
!!
ANIMALS ALL OVER THE EARTH ARE DYING! SOME SPECIES ARE ALREADY GONE FOREVER!
!!!
THE WORLD IS BECOMING SUCH A TERRIBLE PLACE!
?!
BOO! HOO! HOO!
WHY ARE YOU CRYING?
I'M SO SAD! THE WORLD IS GOING TO SHIT!!!
YOU SEE, THERE IS A LOT OF PAIN AND SUFFERING IN THE WORLD.
YEAH! THANKS FOR POINTING IT OUT TO ME!!!

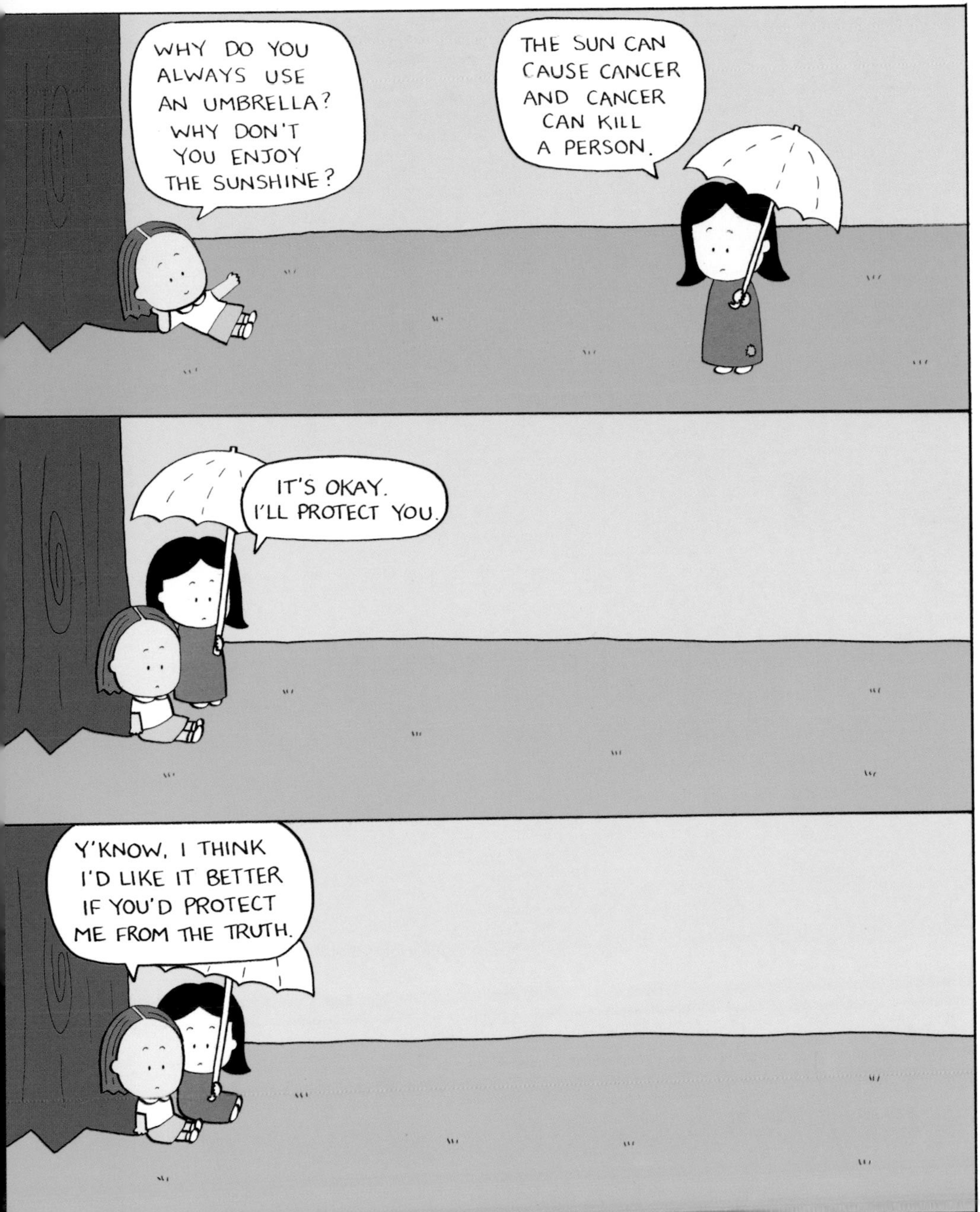
WHY DO YOU ALWAYS USE AN UMBRELLA? WHY DON'T YOU ENJOY THE SUNSHINE?
THE SUN CAN CAUSE CANCER AND CANCER CAN KILL A PERSON.
IT'S OKAY. I'LL PROTECT YOU.
Y'KNOW, I THINK I'D LIKE IT BETTER IF YOU'D PROTECT ME FROM THE TRUTH.

I'm Sorry, So Sorry!

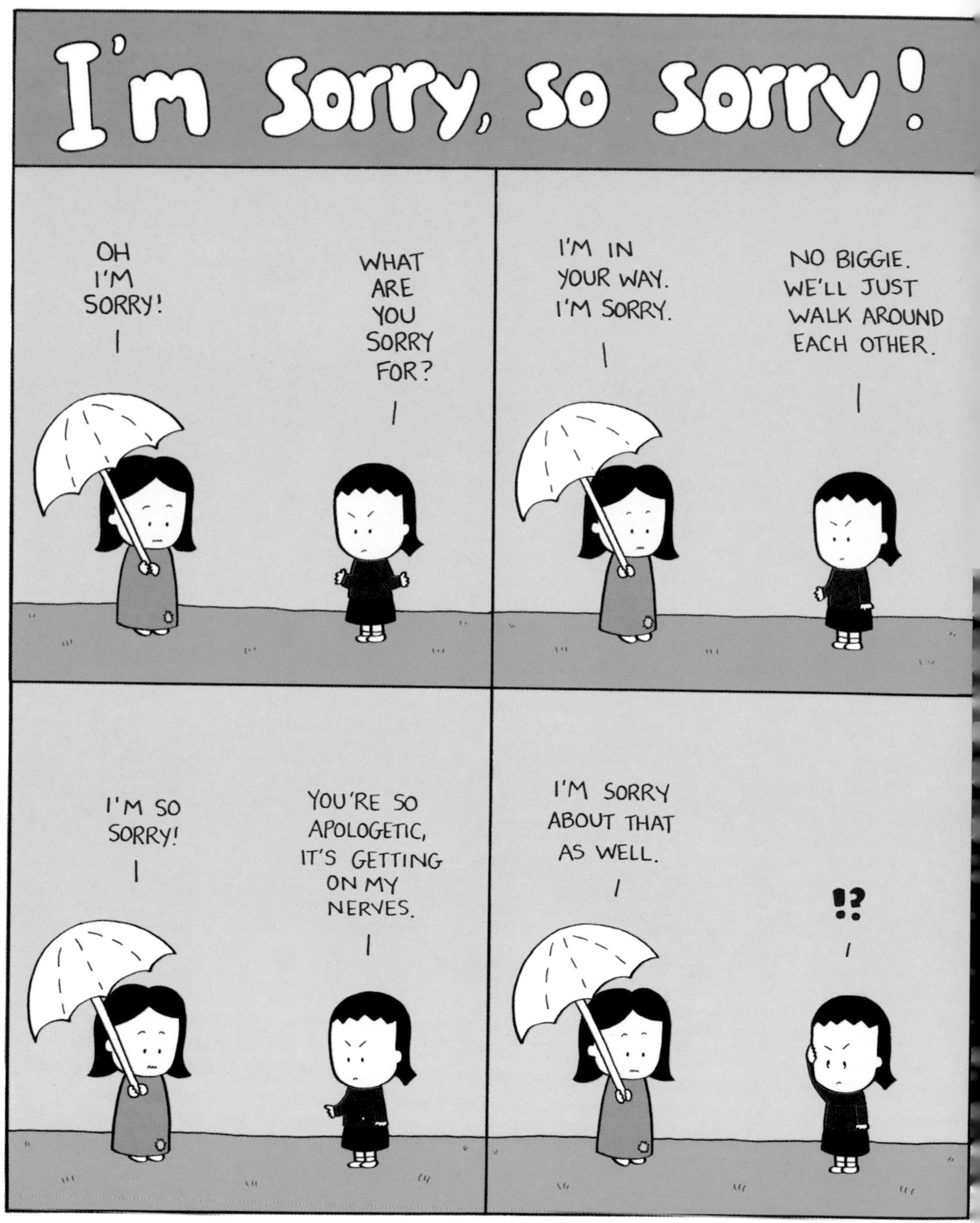
OH I'M SORRY!
WHAT ARE YOU SORRY FOR?
I'M IN YOUR WAY. I'M SORRY.
NO BIGGIE. WE'LL JUST WALK AROUND EACH OTHER.
I'M SO SORRY!
YOU'RE SO APOLOGETIC, IT'S GETTING ON MY NERVES.
I'M SORRY ABOUT THAT AS WELL.
!?

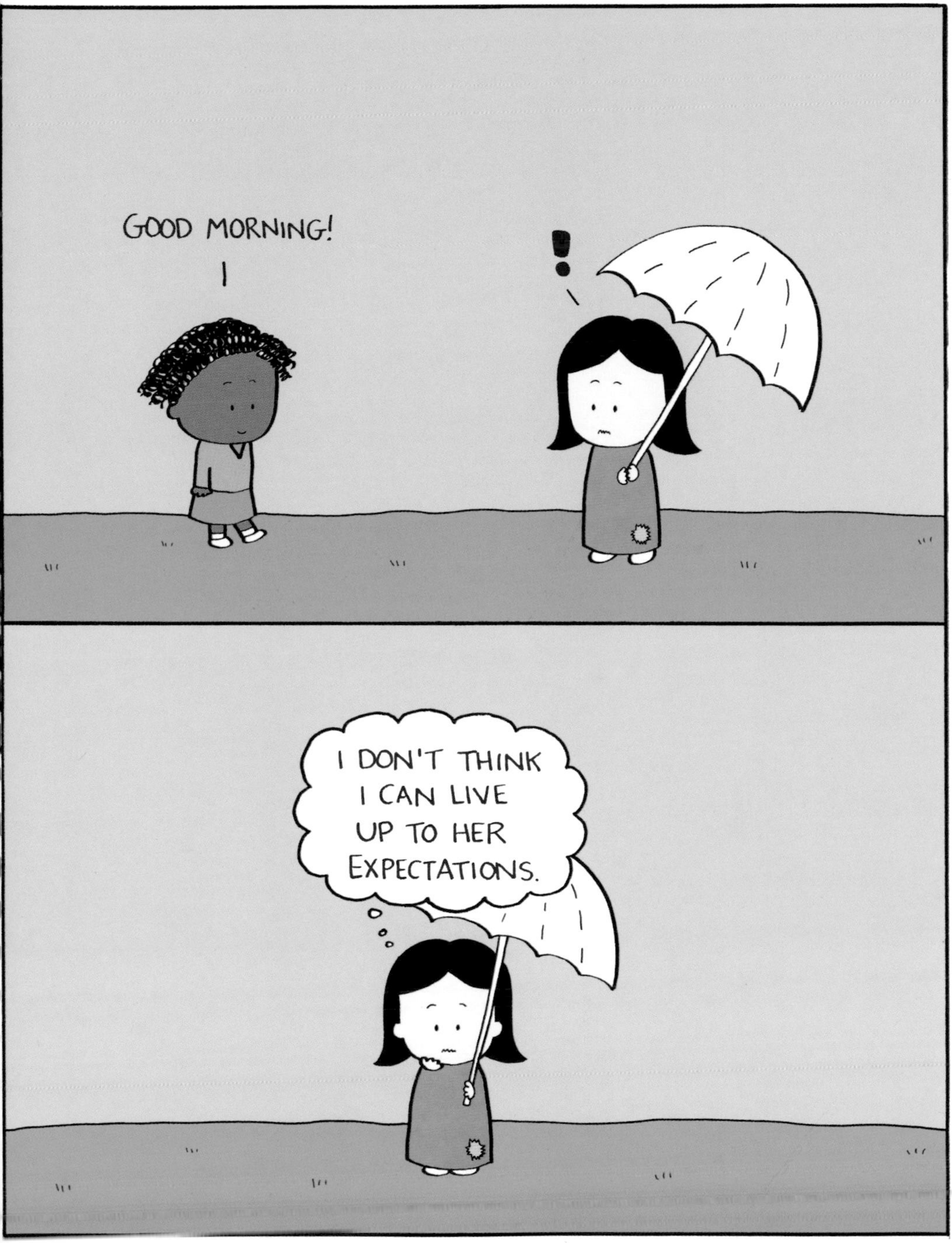
GOOD MORNING!
I DON'T THINK I CAN LIVE UP TO HER EXPECTATIONS.

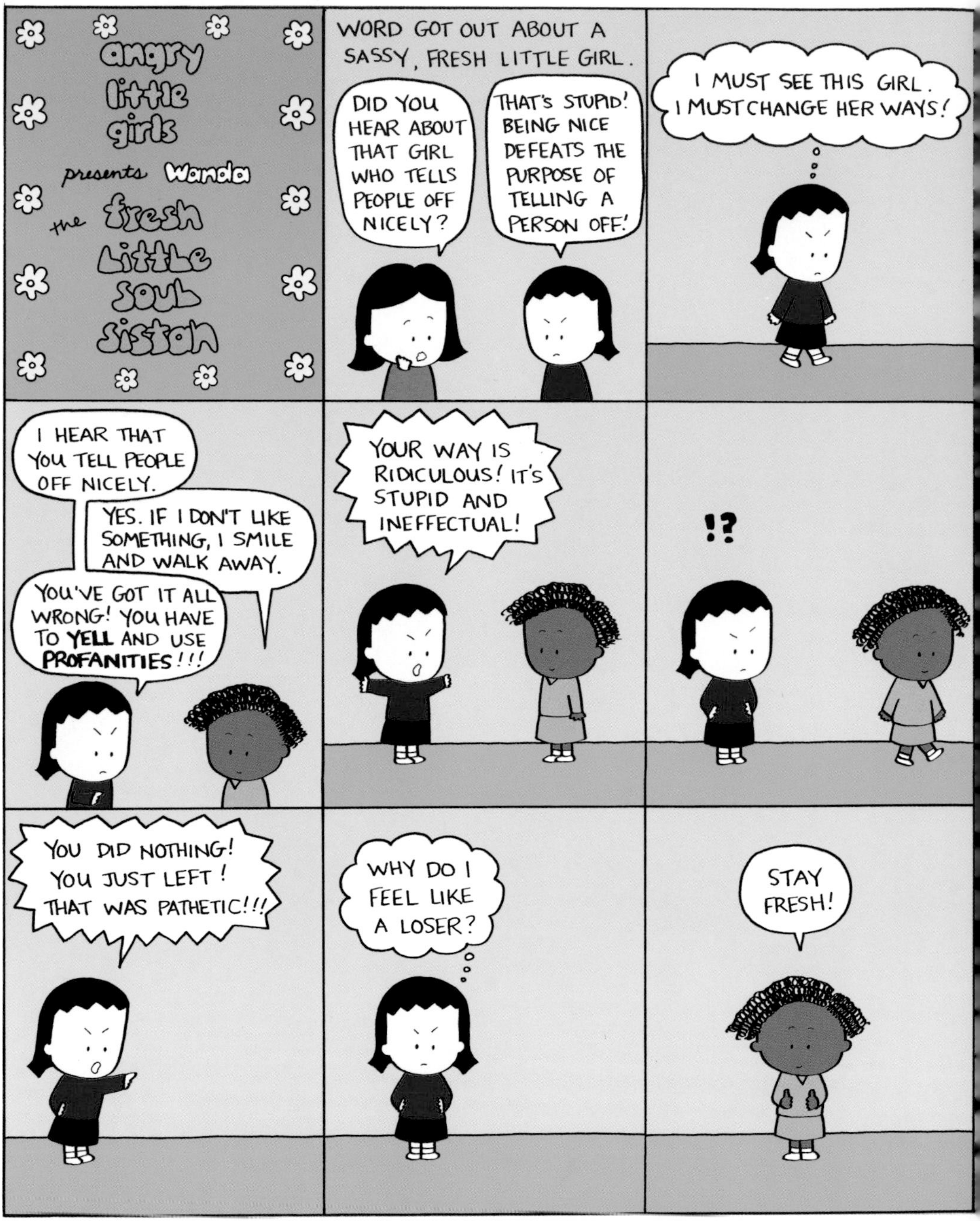
angry little girls presents Wanda the fresh little soul sistah
WORD GOT OUT ABOUT A SASSY, FRESH LITTLE GIRL.
DID YOU HEAR ABOUT THAT GIRL WHO TELLS PEOPLE OFF NICELY?
THAT'S STUPID! BEING NICE DEFEATS THE PURPOSE OF TELLING A PERSON OFF!
I MUST SEE THIS GIRL. I MUST CHANGE HER WAYS!
I HEAR THAT YOU TELL PEOPLE OFF NICELY.
YES. IF I DON'T LIKE SOMETHING, I SMILE AND WALK AWAY.
YOU'VE GOT IT ALL WRONG! YOU HAVE TO YELL AND USE PROFANITIES!!!
YOUR WAY IS RIDICULOUS! IT'S STUPID AND INEFFECTUAL!
!?
YOU DID NOTHING! YOU JUST LEFT! THAT WAS PATHETIC!!!
WHY DO I FEEL LIKE A LOSER?
STAY FRESH!

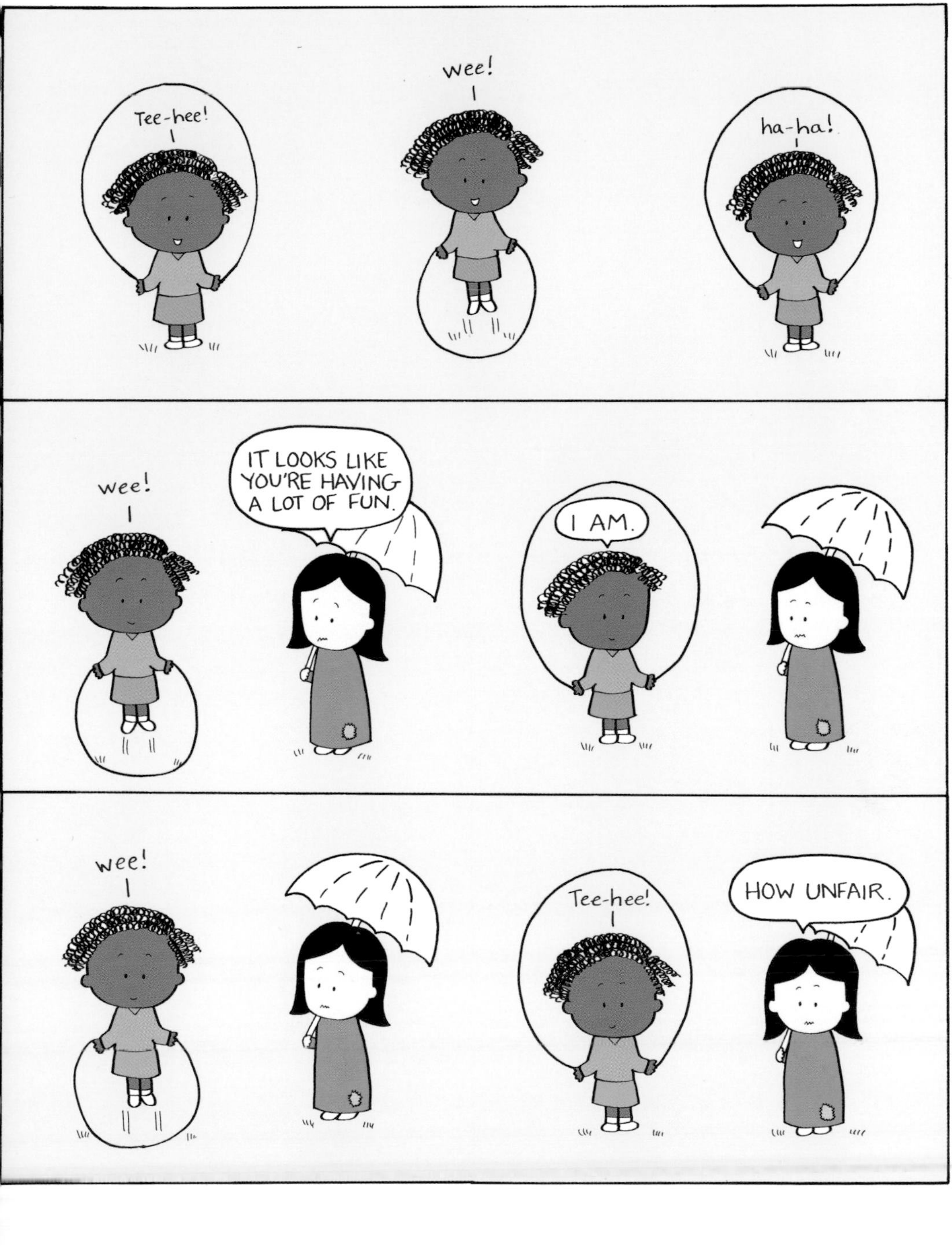
Tee-hee!
wee!
ha-ha!
wee!
IT LOOKS LIKE YOU'RE HAVING A LOT OF FUN.
I AM.
wee!
Tee-hee!
HOW UNFAIR.

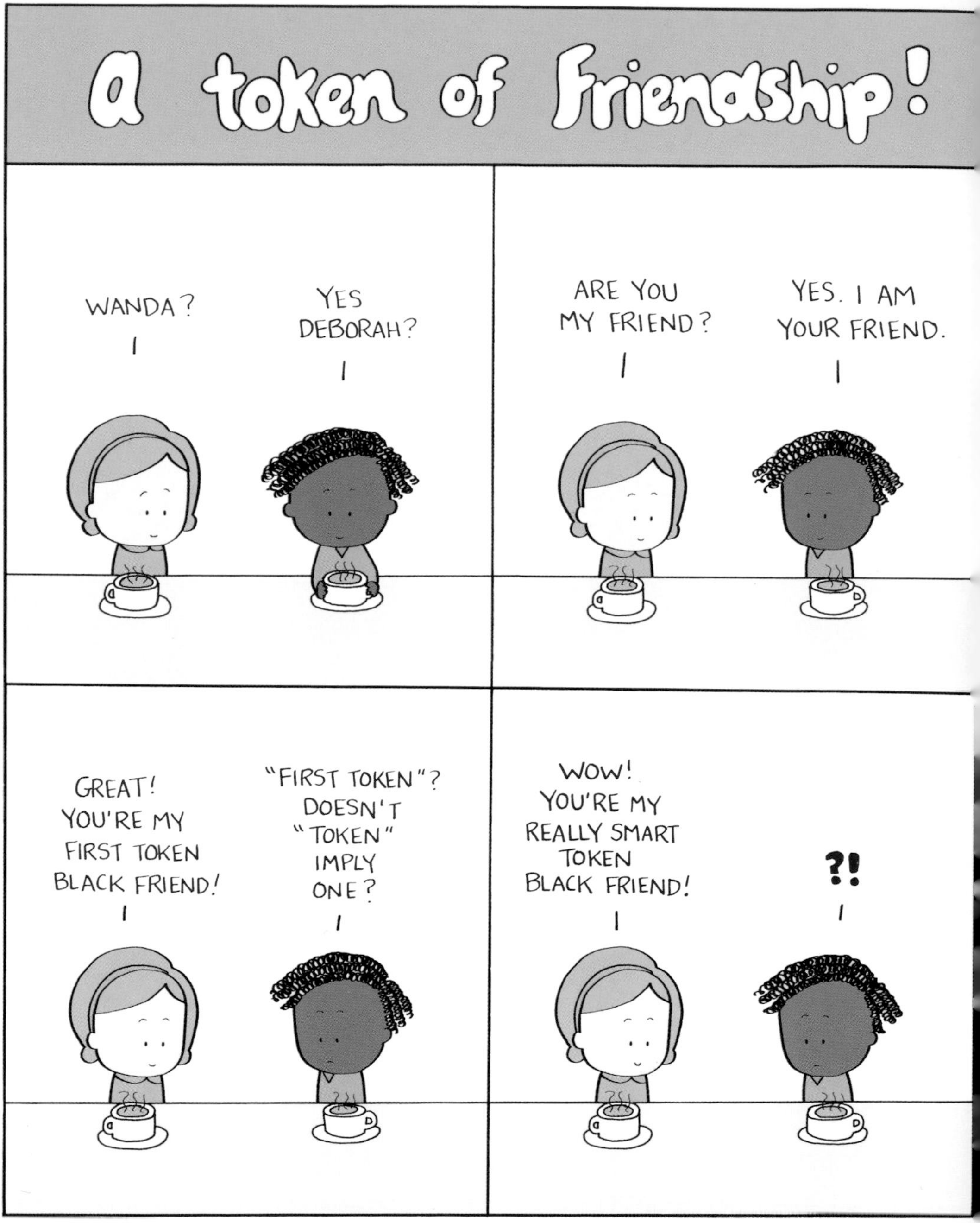
A token of Friendship!
WANDA?
YES DEBORAH?
ARE YOU MY FRIEND?
YES. I AM YOUR FRIEND.
GREAT! YOU'RE MY FIRST TOKEN BLACK FRIEND!
"FIRST TOKEN"? DOESN'T "TOKEN" IMPLY ONE?
WOW! YOU'RE MY REALLY SMART TOKEN BLACK FRIEND!
?!

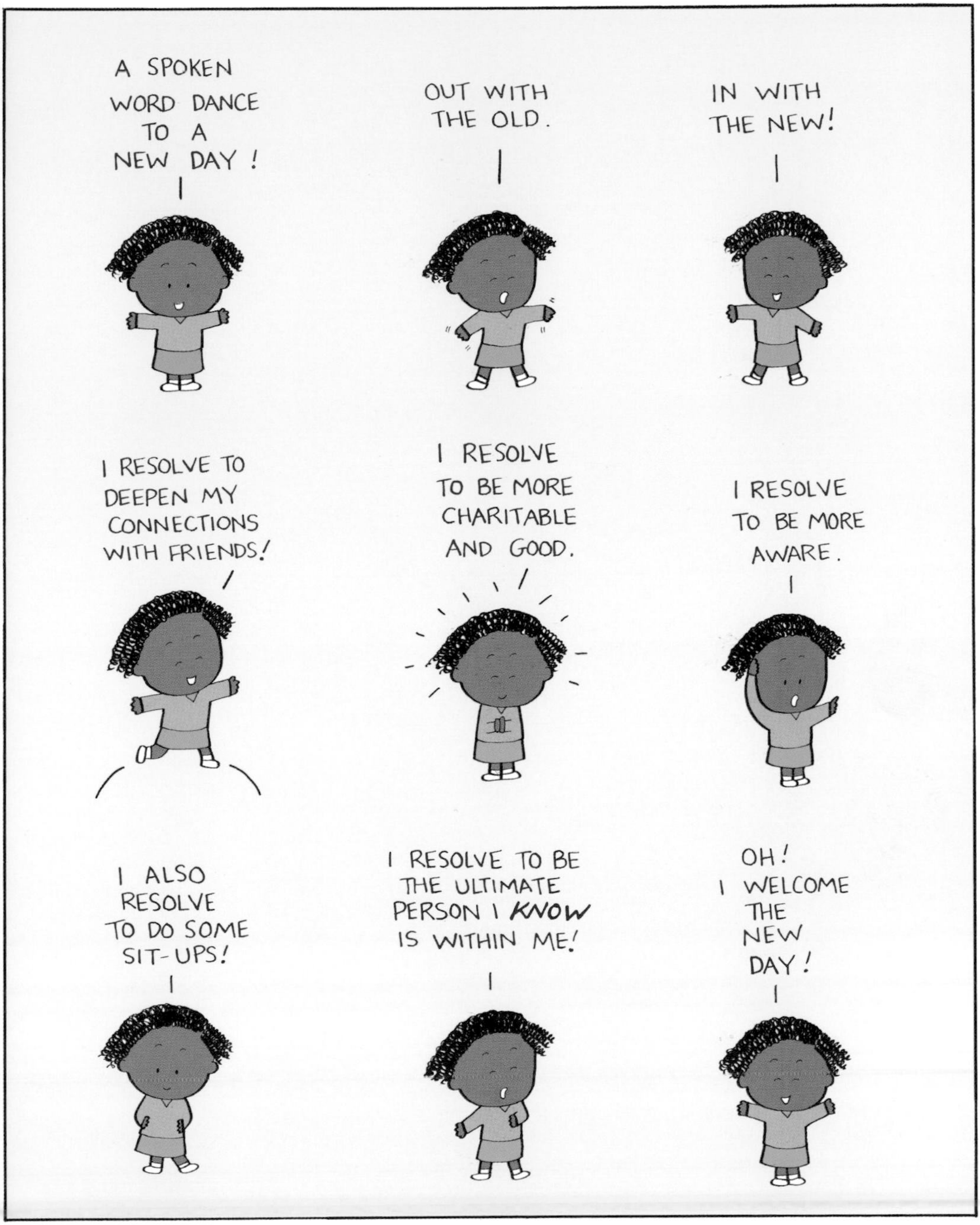

A SPOKEN WORD DANCE TO A NEW DAY!
OUT WITH THE OLD.
IN WITH THE NEW!
I RESOLVE TO DEEPEN MY CONNECTIONS WITH FRIENDS!
I RESOLVE TO BE MORE CHARITABLE AND GOOD.
I RESOLVE TO BE MORE AWARE.
I ALSO RESOLVE TO DO SOME SIT-UPS!
I RESOLVE TO BE THE ULTIMATE PERSON I KNOW IS WITHIN ME!
OH! I WELCOME THE NEW DAY!

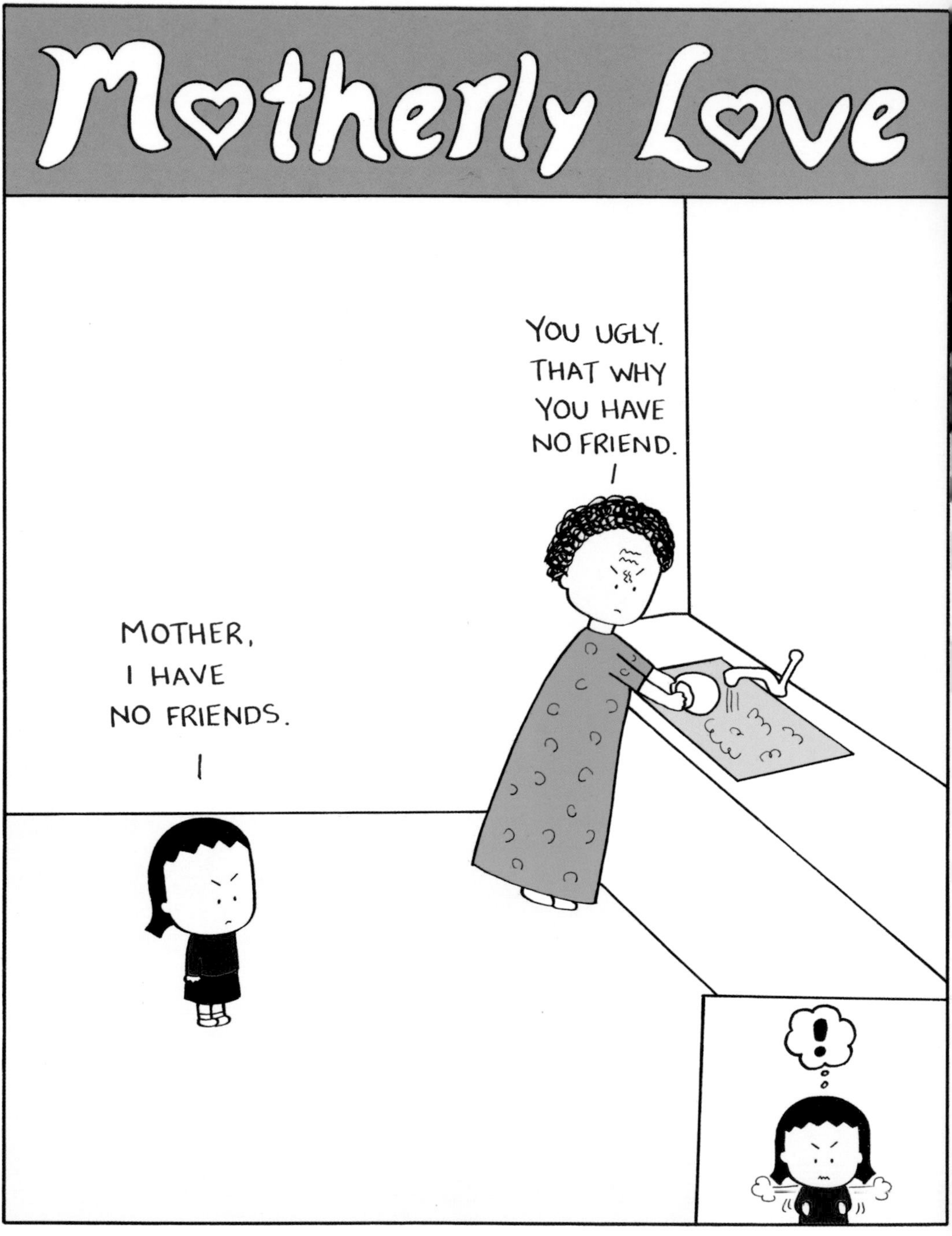
Motherly Love
MOTHER, I HAVE NO FRIENDS.
YOU UGLY. THAT WHY YOU HAVE NO FRIEND.
!

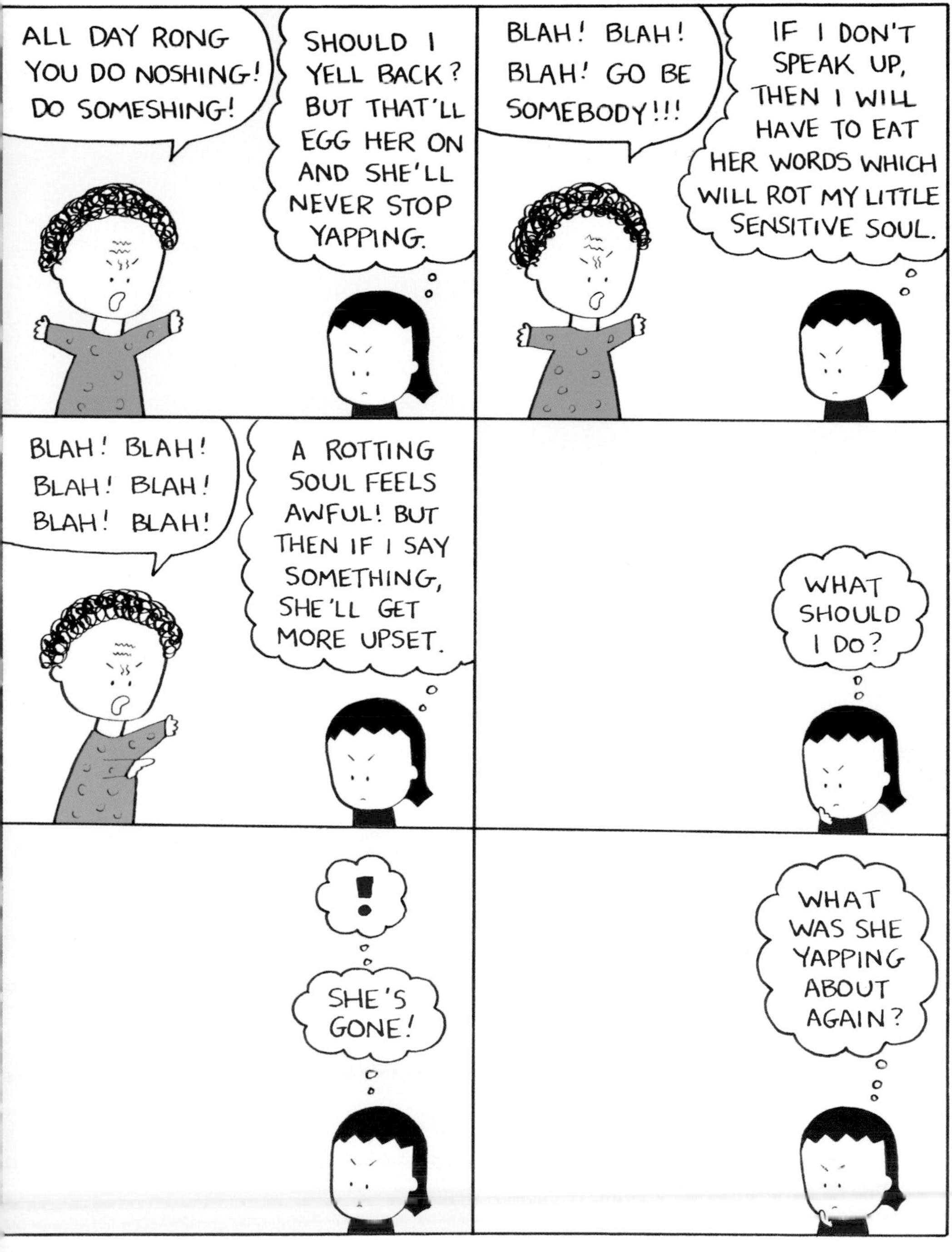
ALL DAY RONG YOU DO NOSHING! DO SOMESHING!
SHOULD I YELL BACK? BUT THAT'LL EGG HER ON AND SHE'LL NEVER STOP YAPPING.
BLAH! BLAH! BLAH! GO BE SOMEBODY!!!
IF I DON'T SPEAK UP, THEN I WILL HAVE TO EAT HER WORDS WHICH WILL ROT MY LITTLE SENSITIVE SOUL.
BLAH! BLAH! BLAH! BLAH! BLAH! BLAH!
A ROTTING SOUL FEELS AWFUL! BUT THEN IF I SAY SOMETHING, SHE'LL GET MORE UPSET.
WHAT SHOULD I DO?
!
SHE'S GONE!
WHAT WAS SHE YAPPING ABOUT AGAIN?

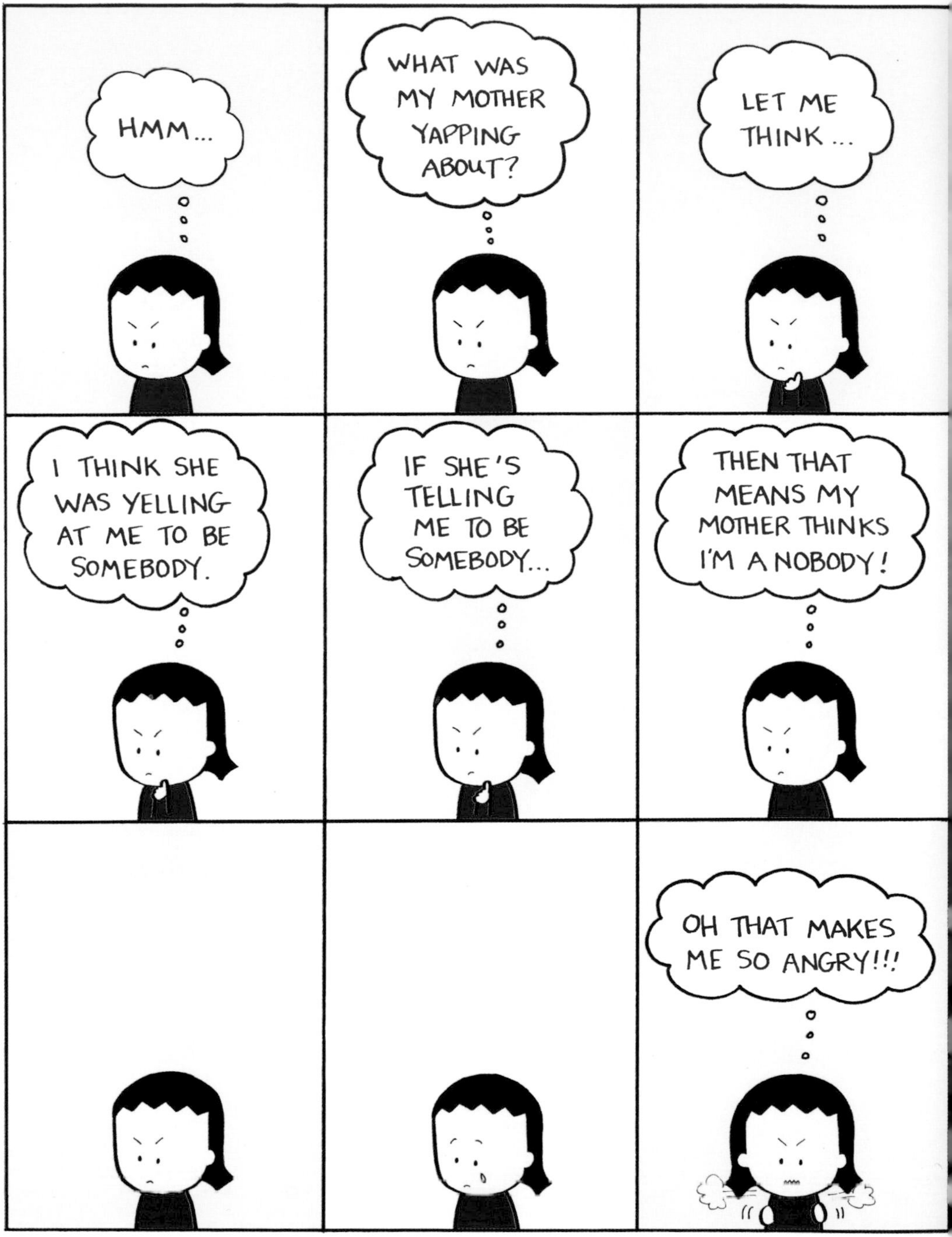
HMM...
WHAT WAS MY MOTHER YAPPING ABOUT?
LET ME THINK...
I THINK SHE WAS YELLING AT ME TO BE SOMEBODY.
IF SHE'S TELLING ME TO BE SOMEBODY...
THEN THAT MEANS MY MOTHER THINKS I'M A NOBODY!
OH THAT MAKES ME SO ANGRY!!!

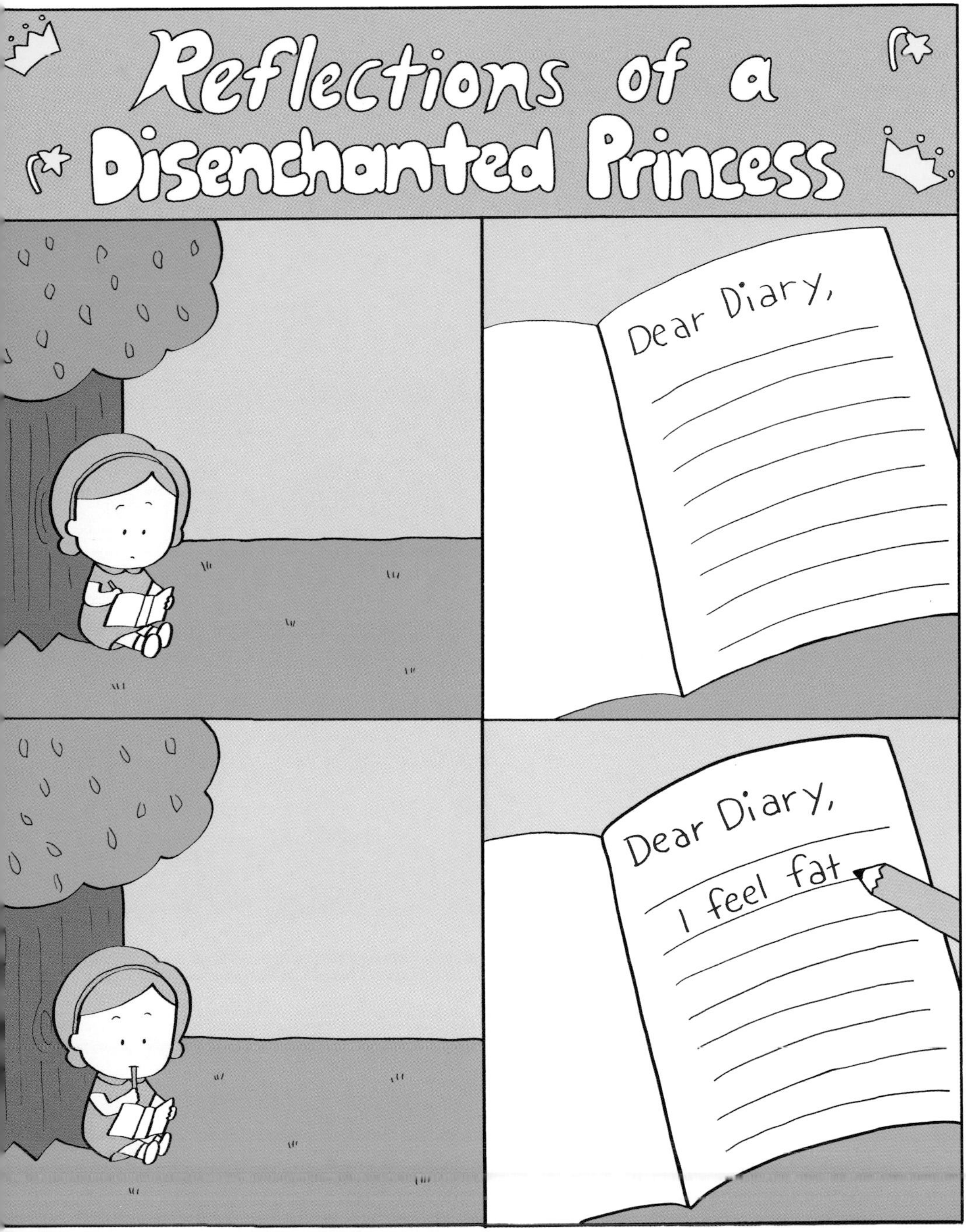
Reflections of a Disenchanted Princess
Dear Diary,
Dear Diary,
I feel fat

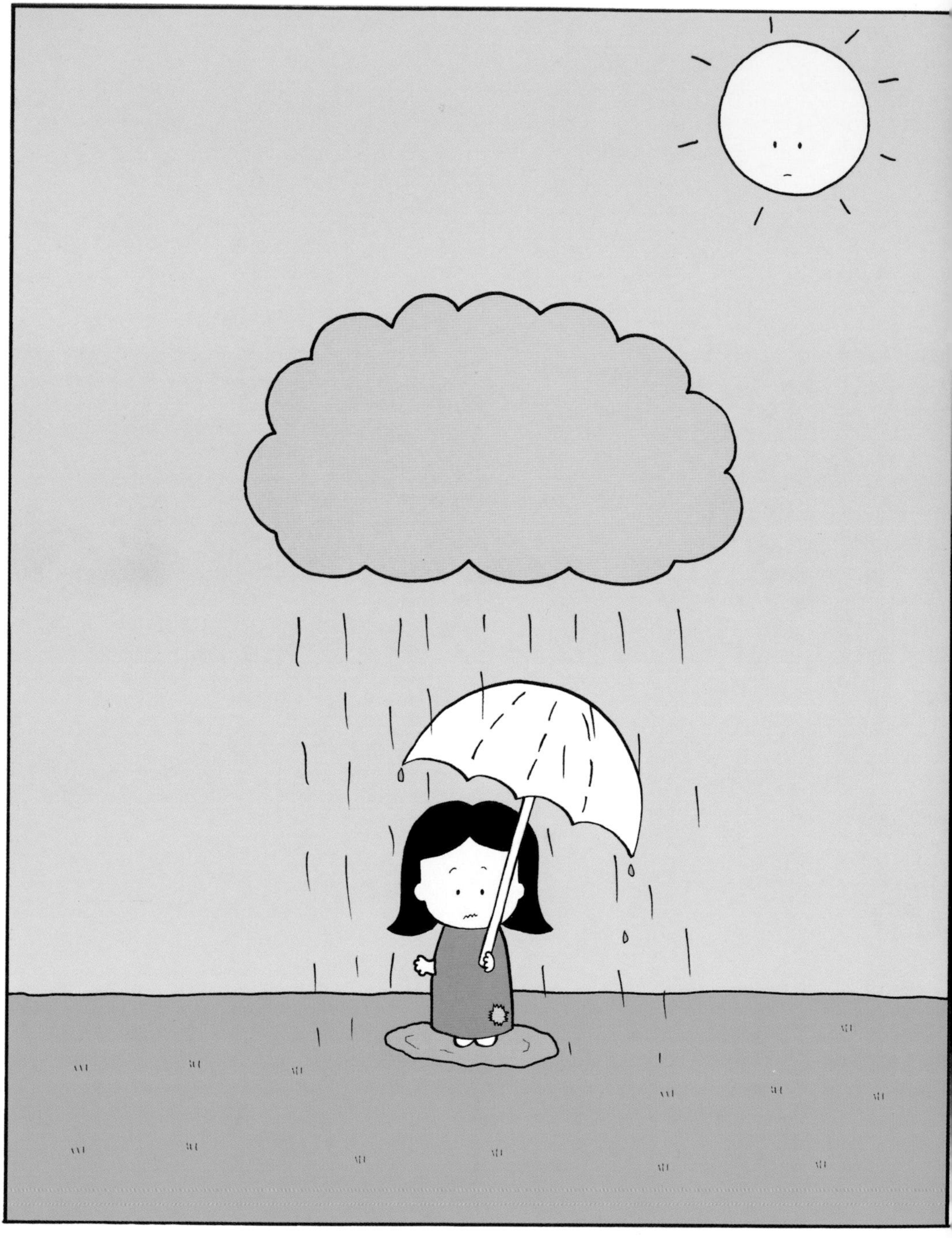

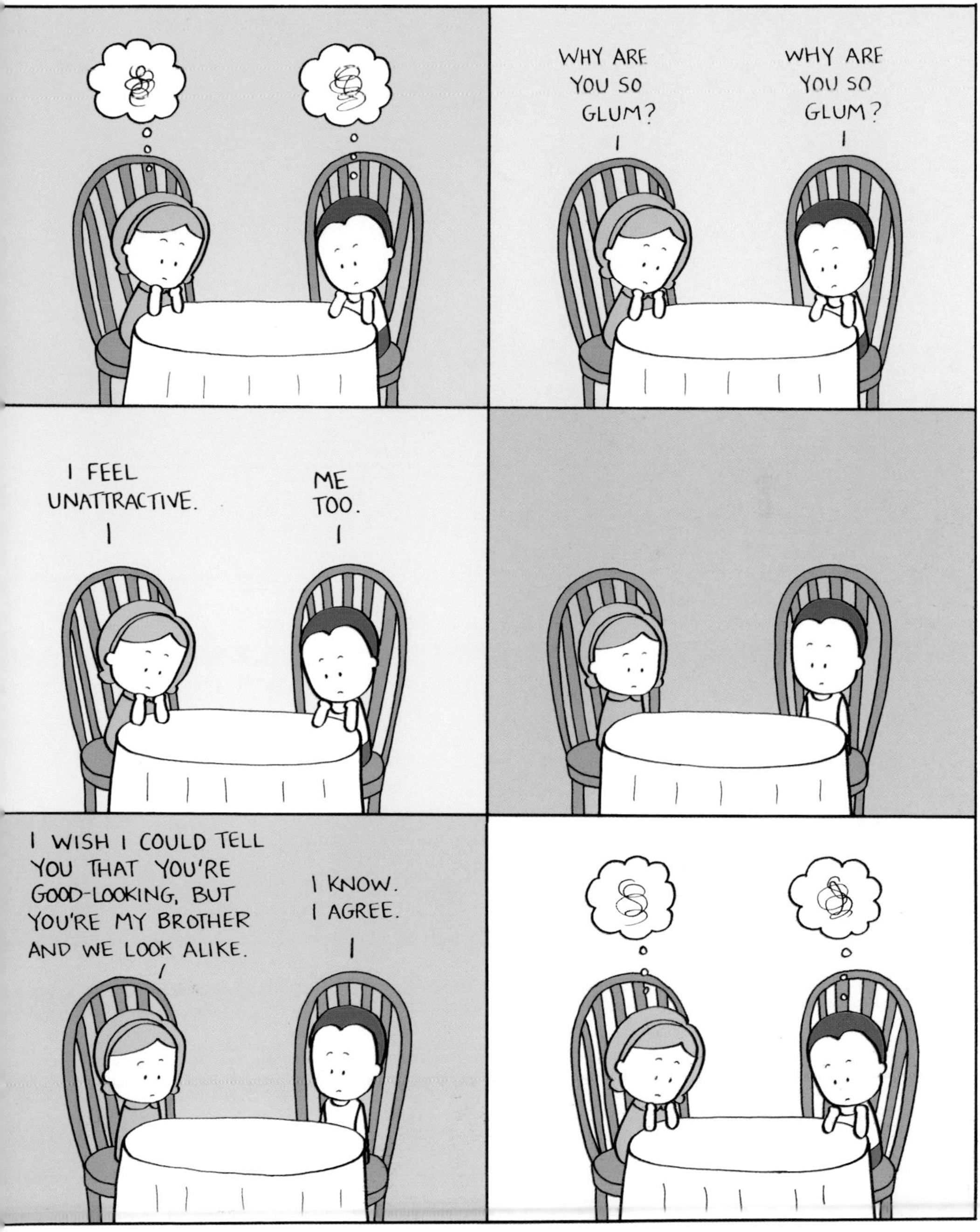
WHY ARE YOU SO GLUM?
WHY ARE YOU SO GLUM?
I FEEL UNATTRACTIVE.
ME TOO.
I WISH I COULD TELL YOU THAT YOU'RE GOOD-LOOKING, BUT YOU'RE MY BROTHER AND WE LOOK ALIKE.
I KNOW. I AGREE.

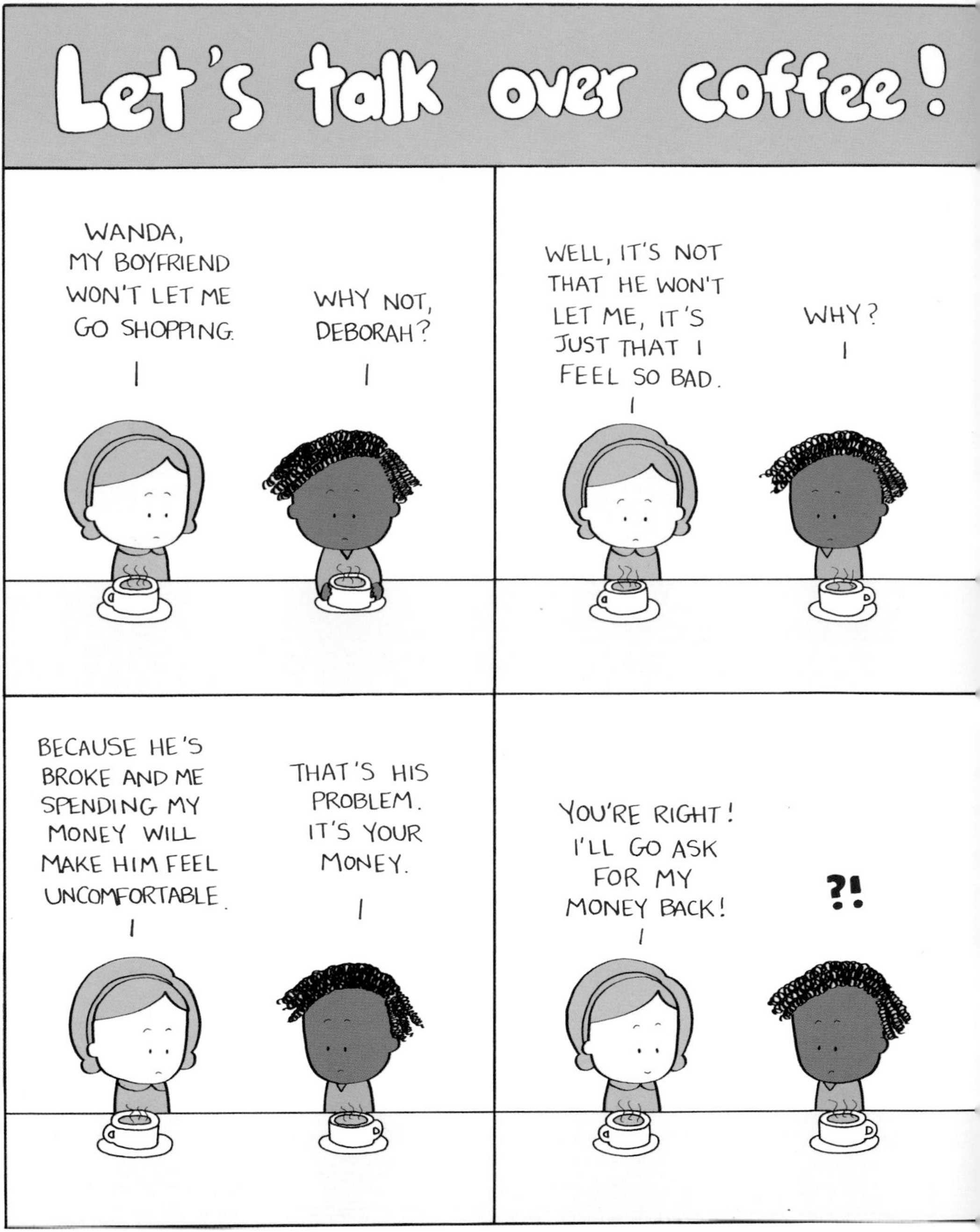
Let's talk over coffee!
WANDA, MY BOYFRIEND WON'T LET ME GO SHOPPING.
WHY NOT, DEBORAH?
WELL, IT'S NOT THAT HE WON'T LET ME, IT'S JUST THAT I FEEL SO BAD.
WHY?
BECAUSE HE'S BROKE AND ME SPENDING MY MONEY WILL MAKE HIM FEEL UNCOMFORTABLE.
THAT'S HIS PROBLEM. IT'S YOUR MONEY.
YOU'RE RIGHT! I'LL GO ASK FOR MY MONEY BACK!
?!

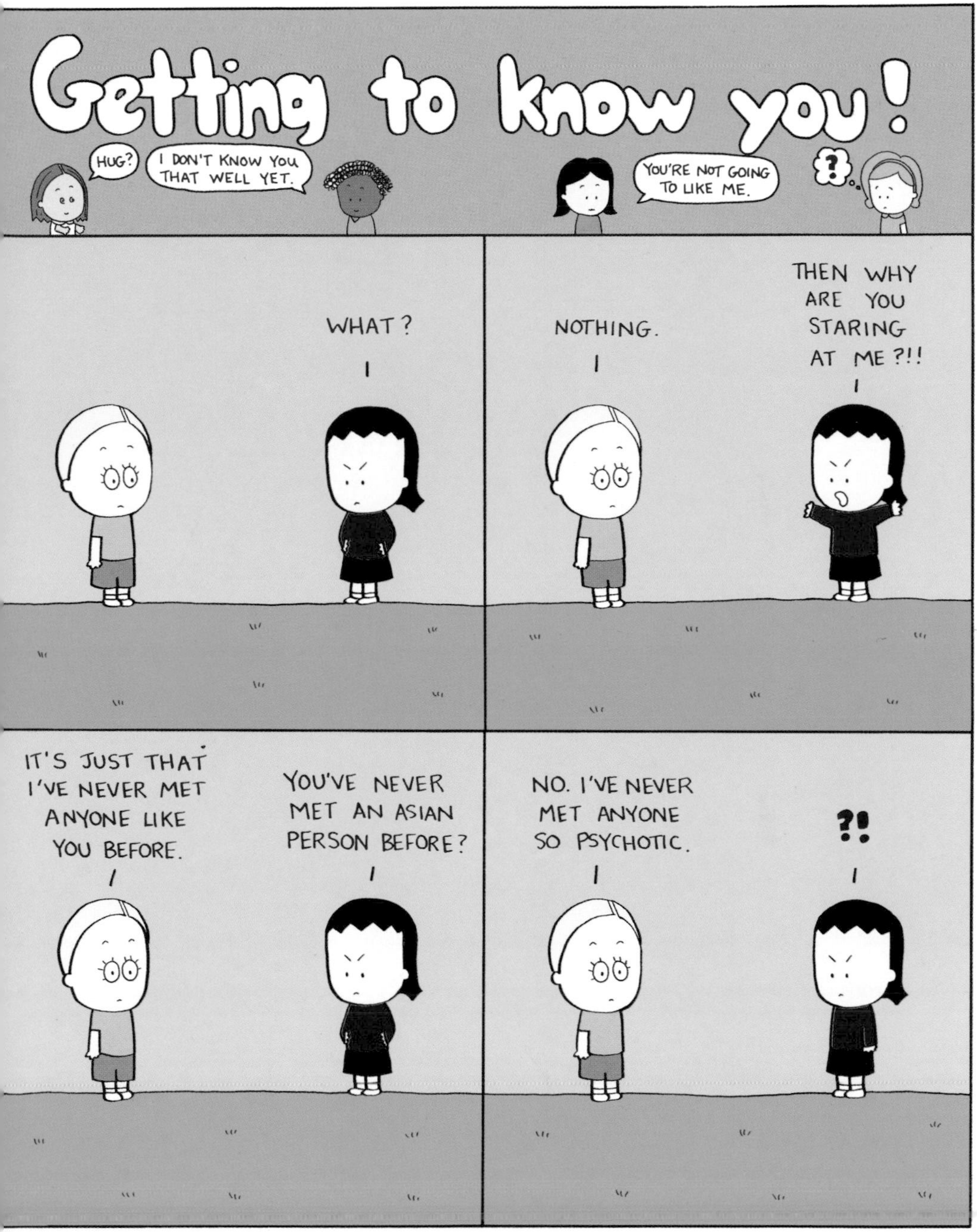
Getting to know you!
HUG?
I DON'T KNOW YOU THAT WELL YET.
YOU'RE NOT GOING TO LIKE ME.
?
WHAT?
NOTHING.
THEN WHY ARE YOU STARING AT ME?!!
IT'S JUST THAT I'VE NEVER MET ANYONE LIKE YOU BEFORE.
YOU'VE NEVER MET AN ASIAN PERSON BEFORE?
NO. I'VE NEVER MET ANYONE SO PSYCHOTIC.
?!

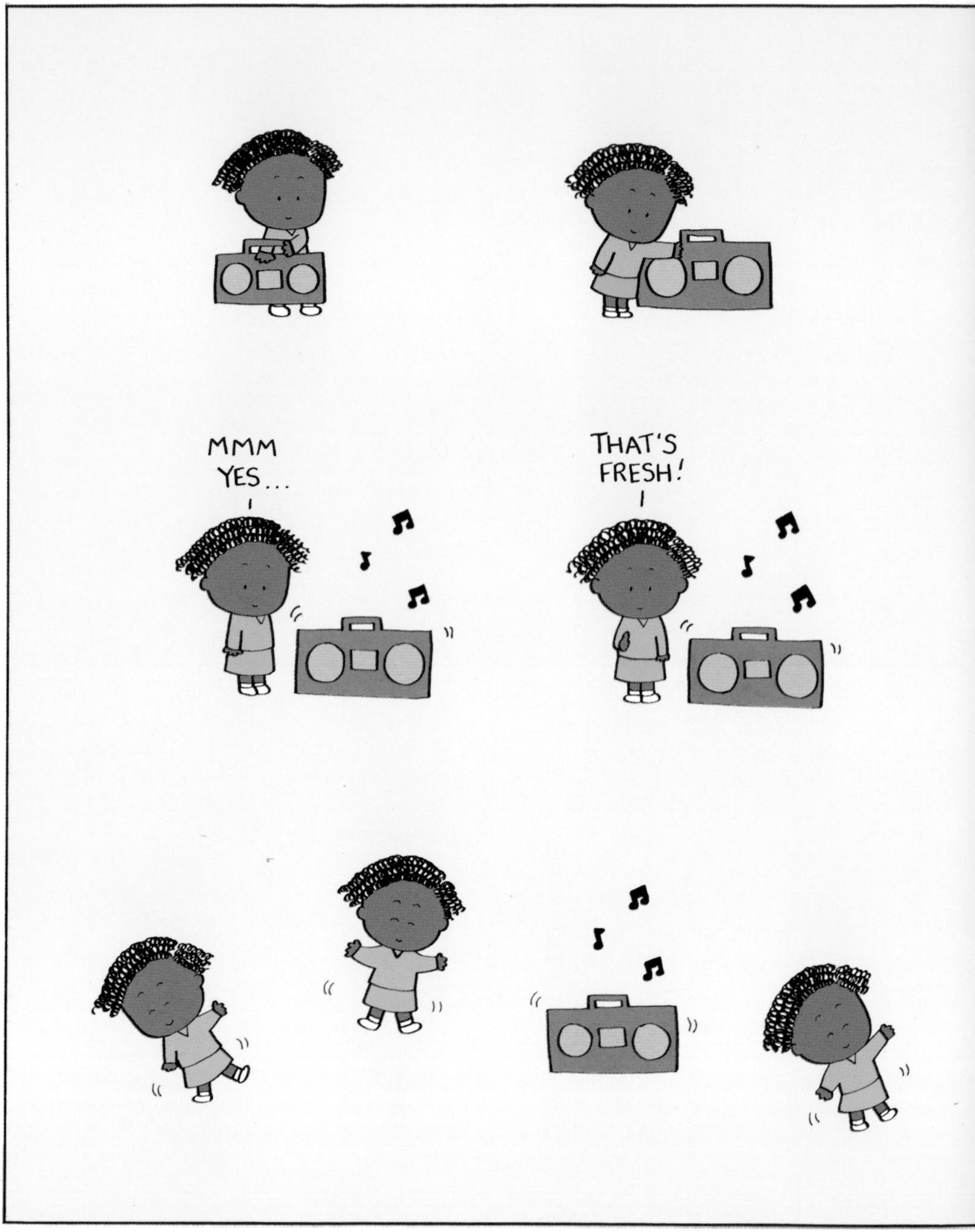
MMM YES...
THAT'S FRESH!

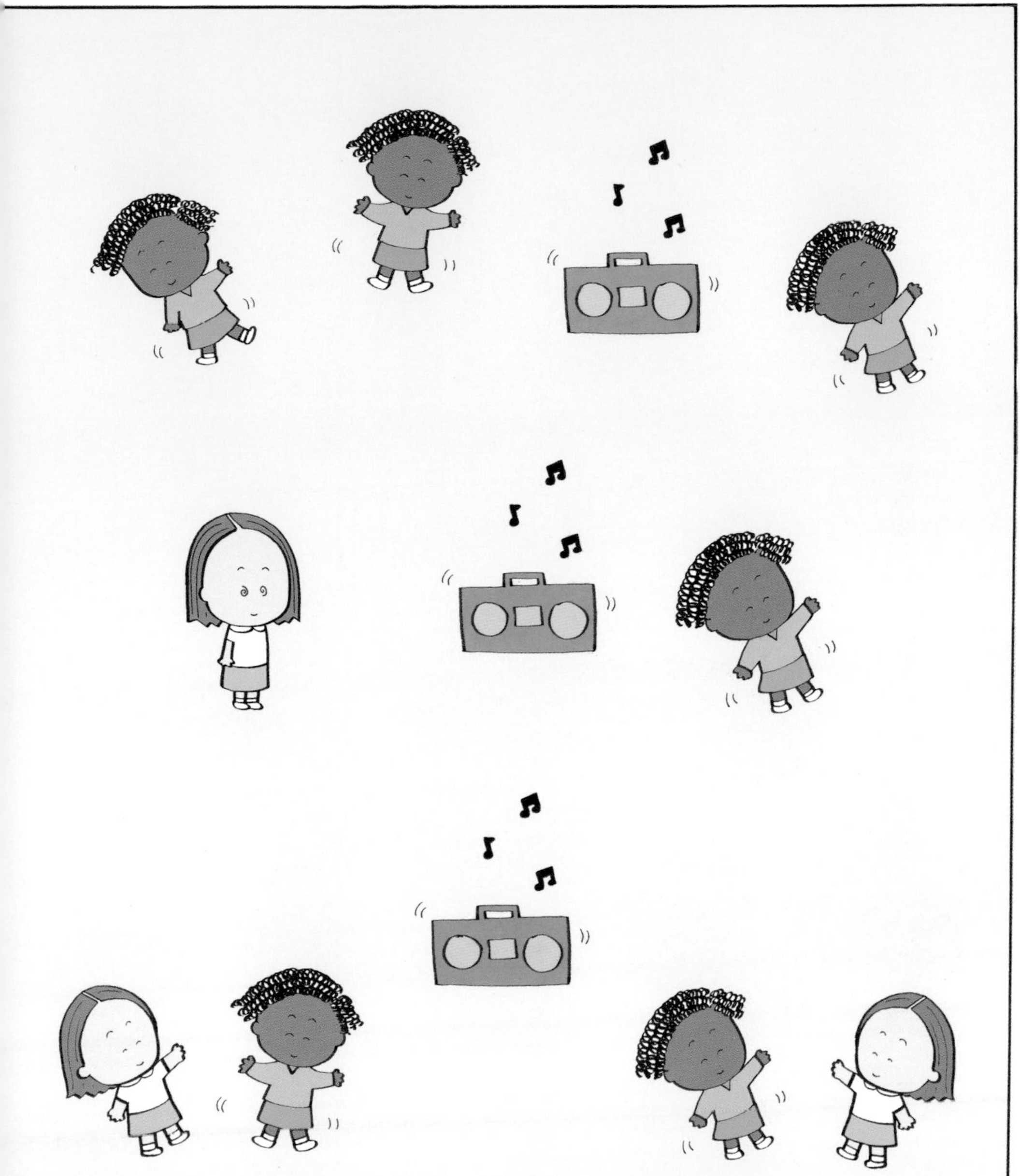

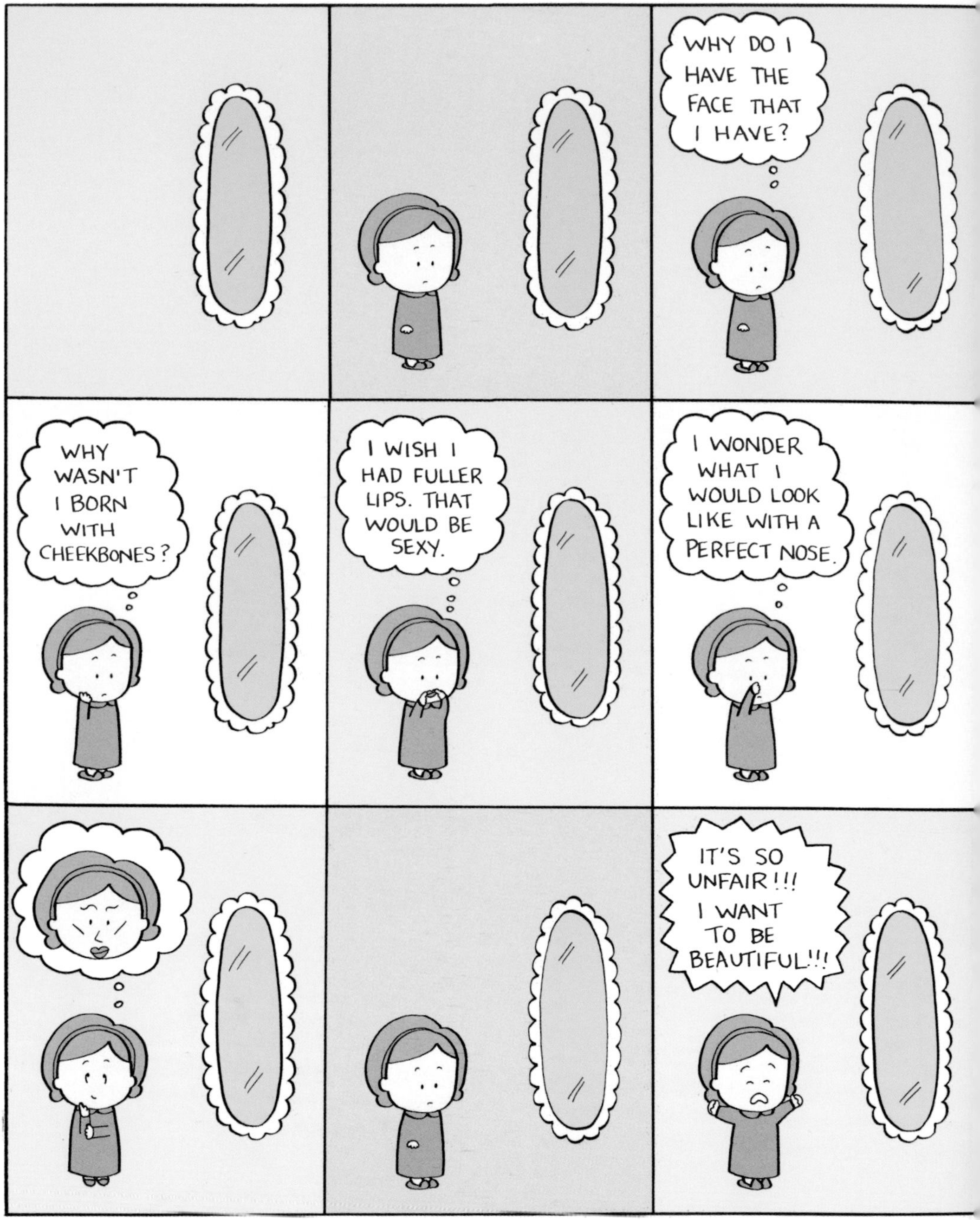
WHY DO I HAVE THE FACE THAT I HAVE?
WHY WASN'T I BORN WITH CHEEKBONES?
I WISH I HAD FULLER LIPS. THAT WOULD BE SEXY.
I WONDER WHAT I WOULD LOOK LIKE WITH A PERFECT NOSE.
IT'S SO UNFAIR!!! I WANT TO BE BEAUTIFUL!!!

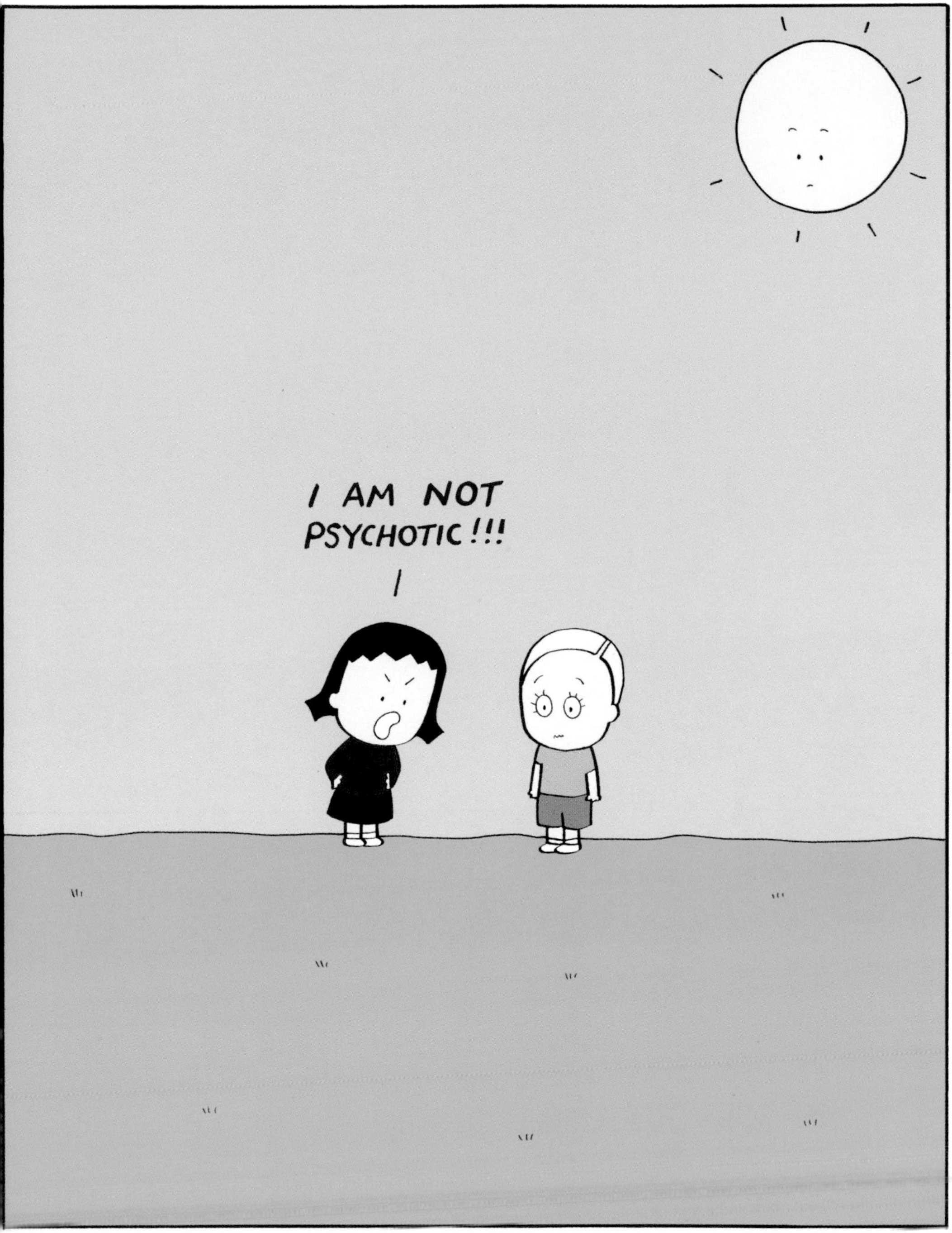
I AM NOT PSYCHOTIC!!!

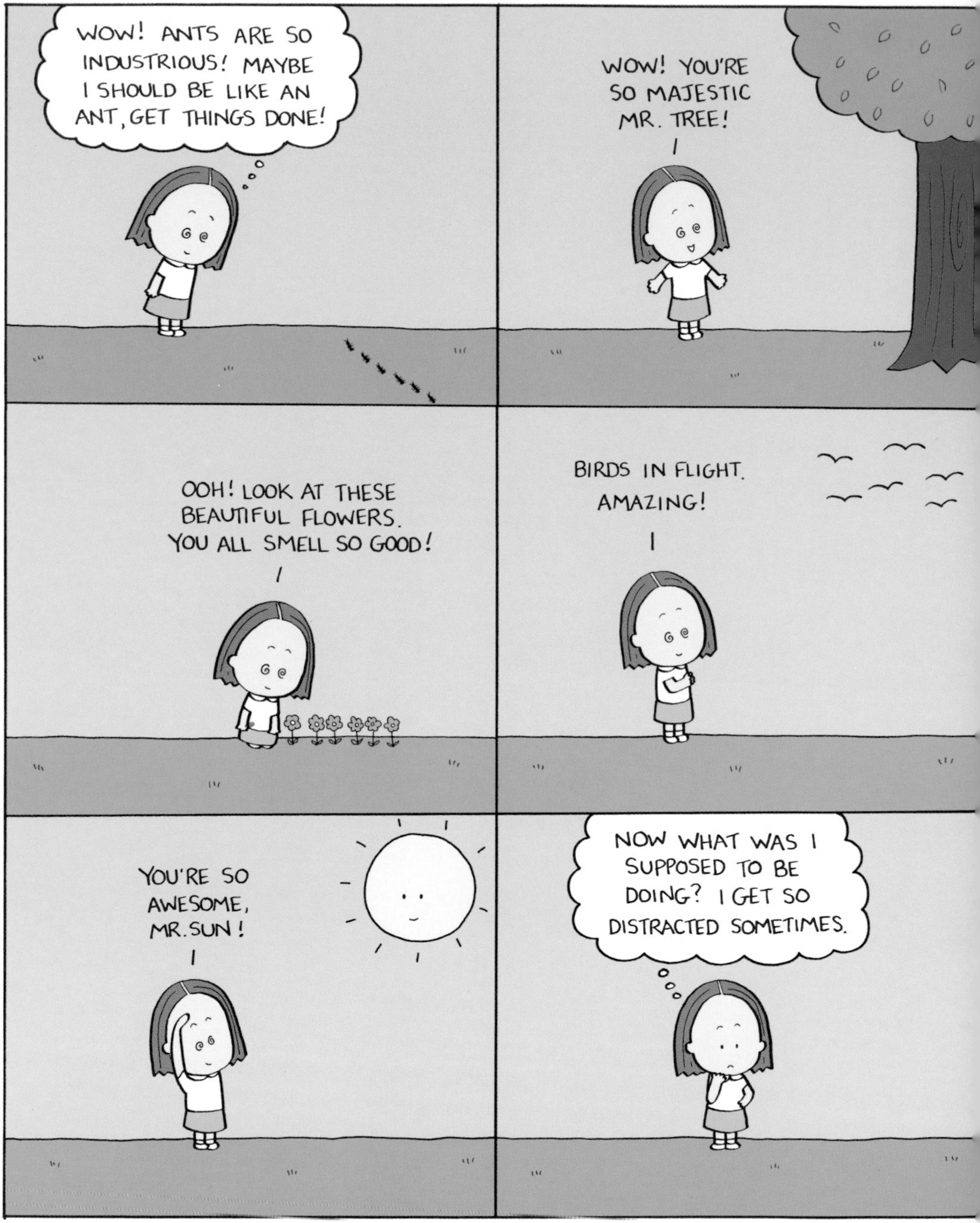
WOW! ANTS ARE SO INDUSTRIOUS! MAYBE I SHOULD BE LIKE AN ANT, GET THINGS DONE!
WOW! YOU'RE SO MAJESTIC MR. TREE!
OOH! LOOK AT THESE BEAUTIFUL FLOWERS. YOU ALL SMELL SO GOOD!
BIRDS IN FLIGHT. AMAZING!
YOU'RE SO AWESOME, MR. SUN!
NOW WHAT WAS I SUPPOSED TO BE DOING? I GET SO DISTRACTED SOMETIMES.

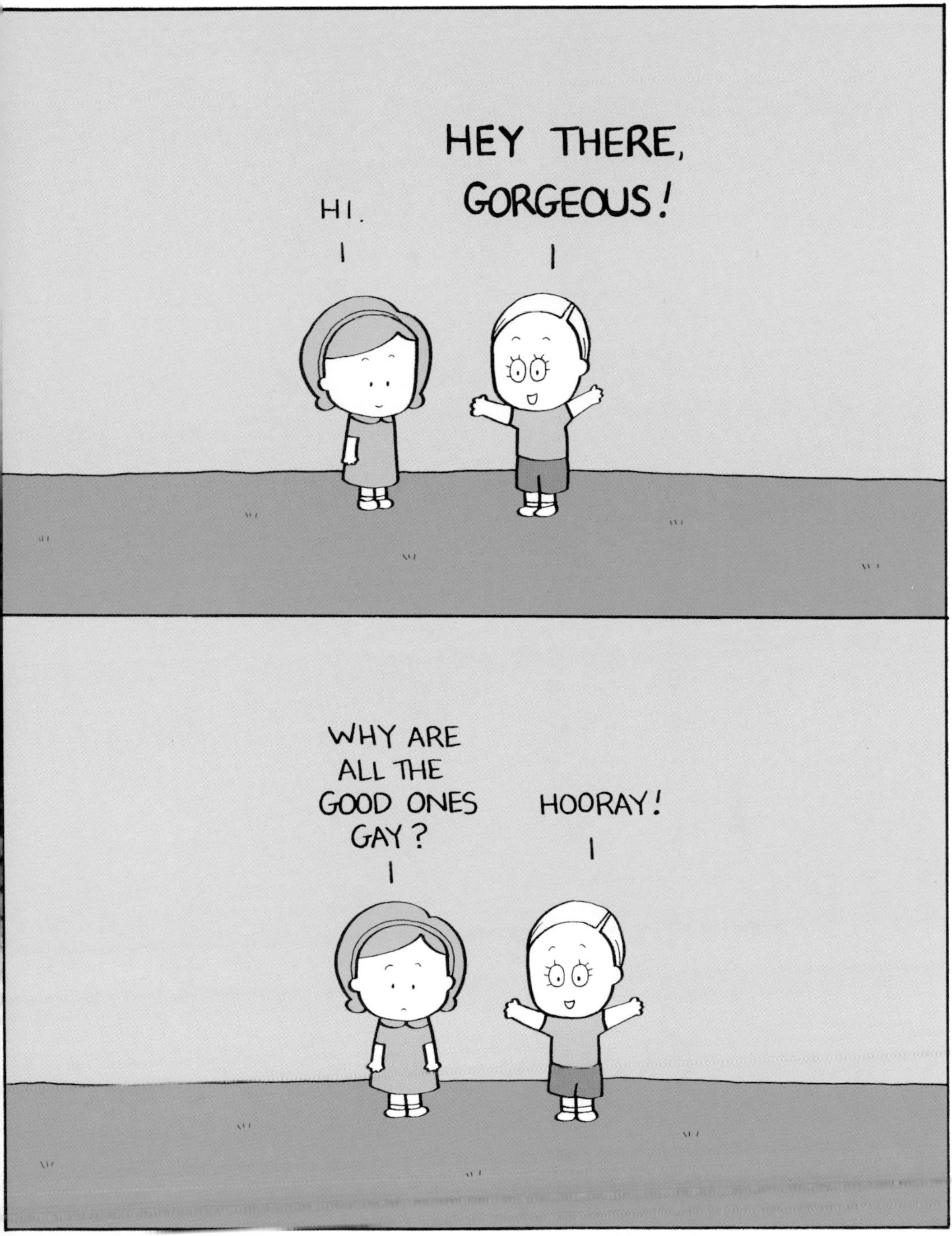
HI.
HEY THERE, GORGEOUS!
WHY ARE ALL THE GOOD ONES GAY?
HOORAY!

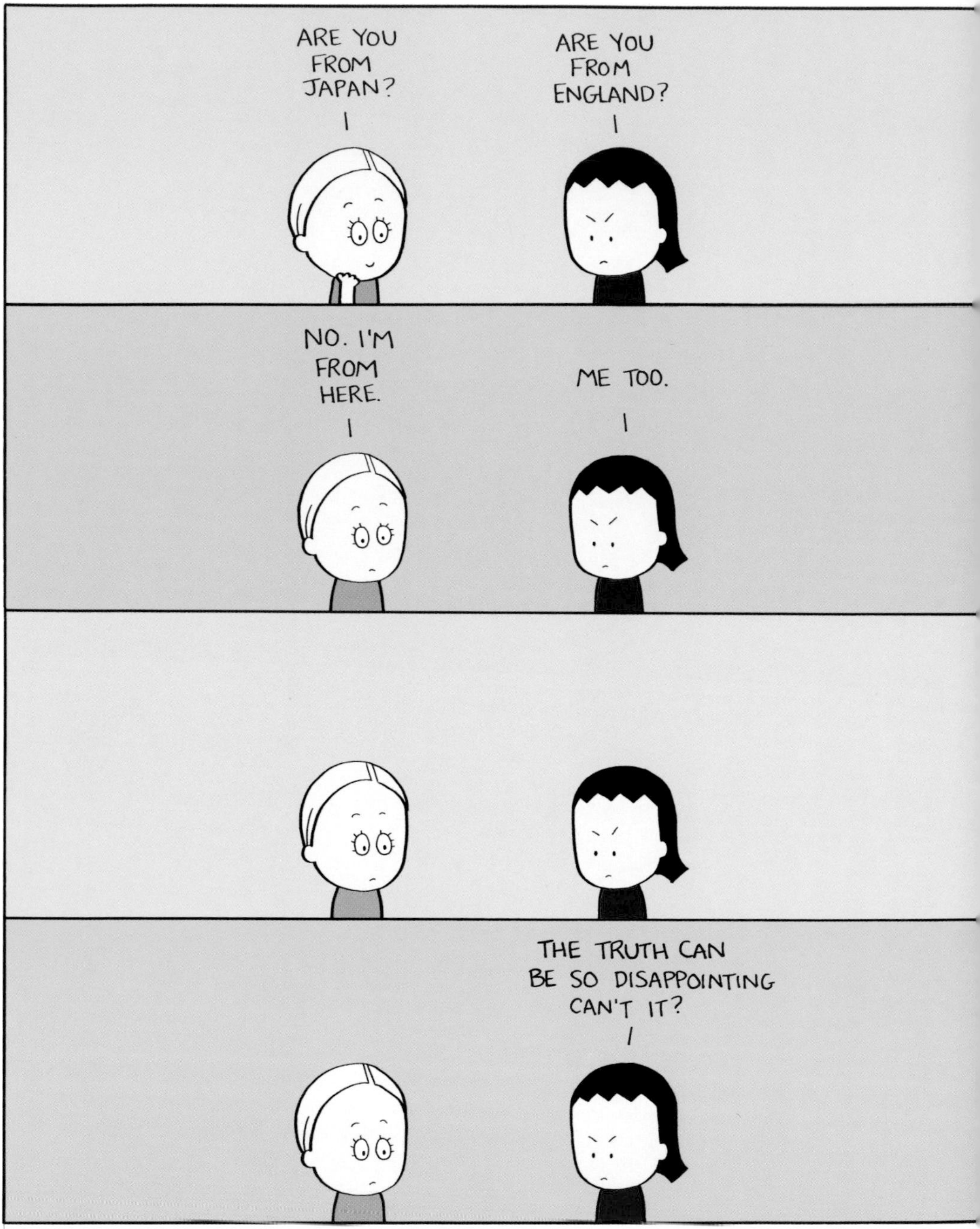
ARE YOU FROM JAPAN?
ARE YOU FROM ENGLAND?
NO. I'M FROM HERE.
ME TOO.
THE TRUTH CAN BE SO DISAPPOINTING CAN'T IT?

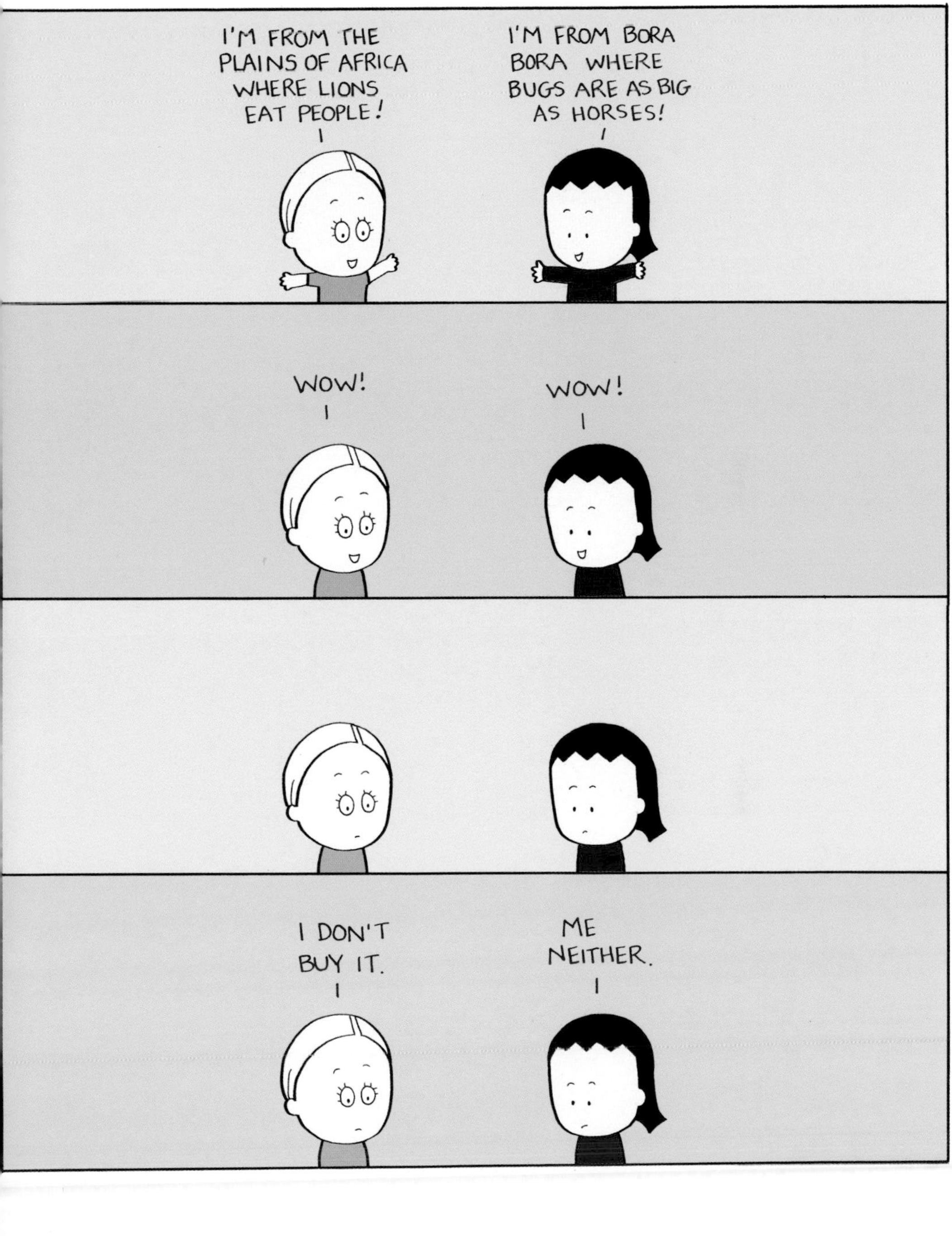
I'M FROM THE PLAINS OF AFRICA WHERE LIONS EAT PEOPLE!
I'M FROM BORA BORA WHERE BUGS ARE AS BIG AS HORSES!
WOW!
WOW!
I DON'T BUY IT.
ME NEITHER.

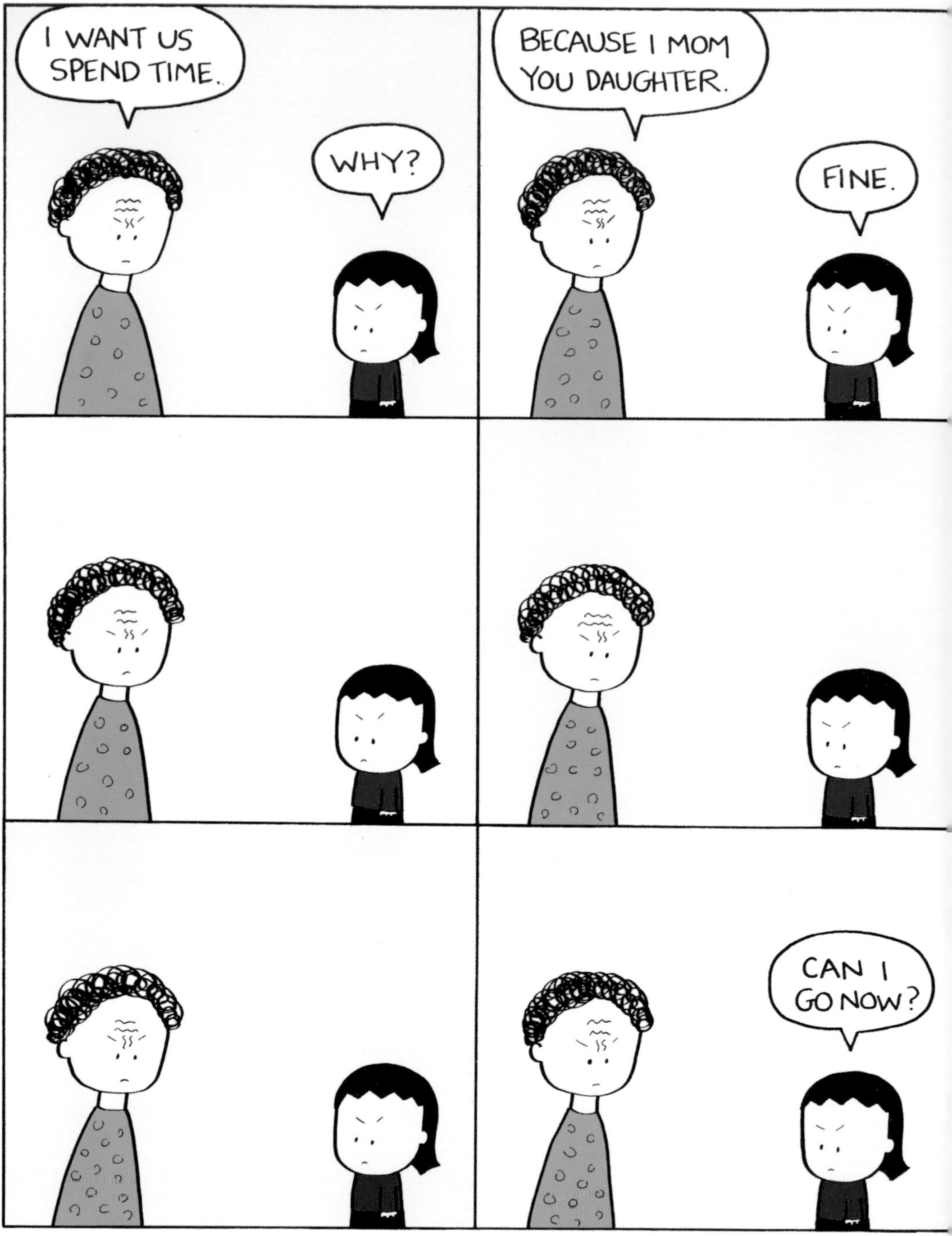
I WANT US SPEND TIME.
WHY?
BECAUSE I MOM YOU DAUGHTER.
FINE.
CAN I GO NOW?

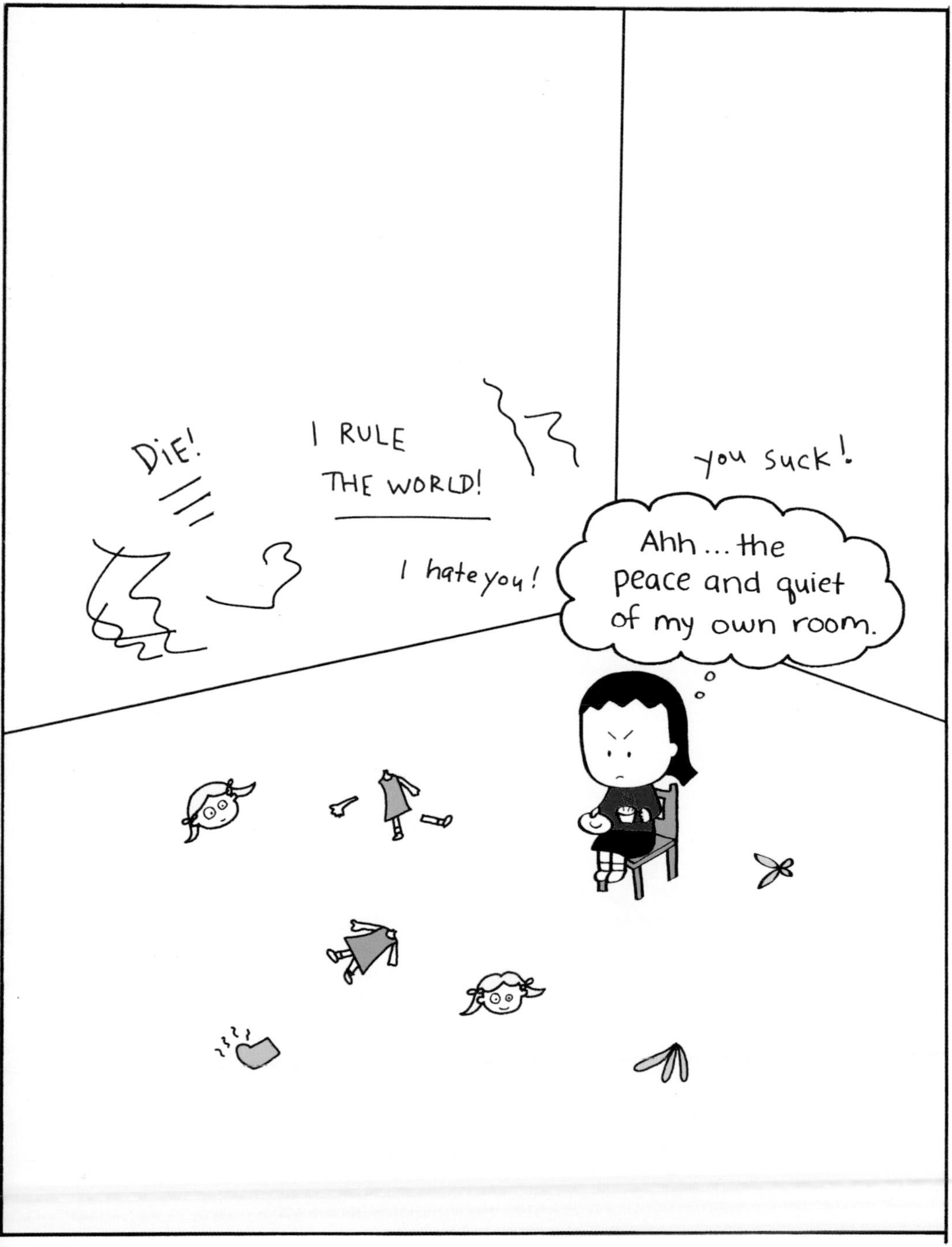
DiE!
I RULE THE WORLD!
I hate you!
you suck!
Ahh... the peace and quiet of my own room.

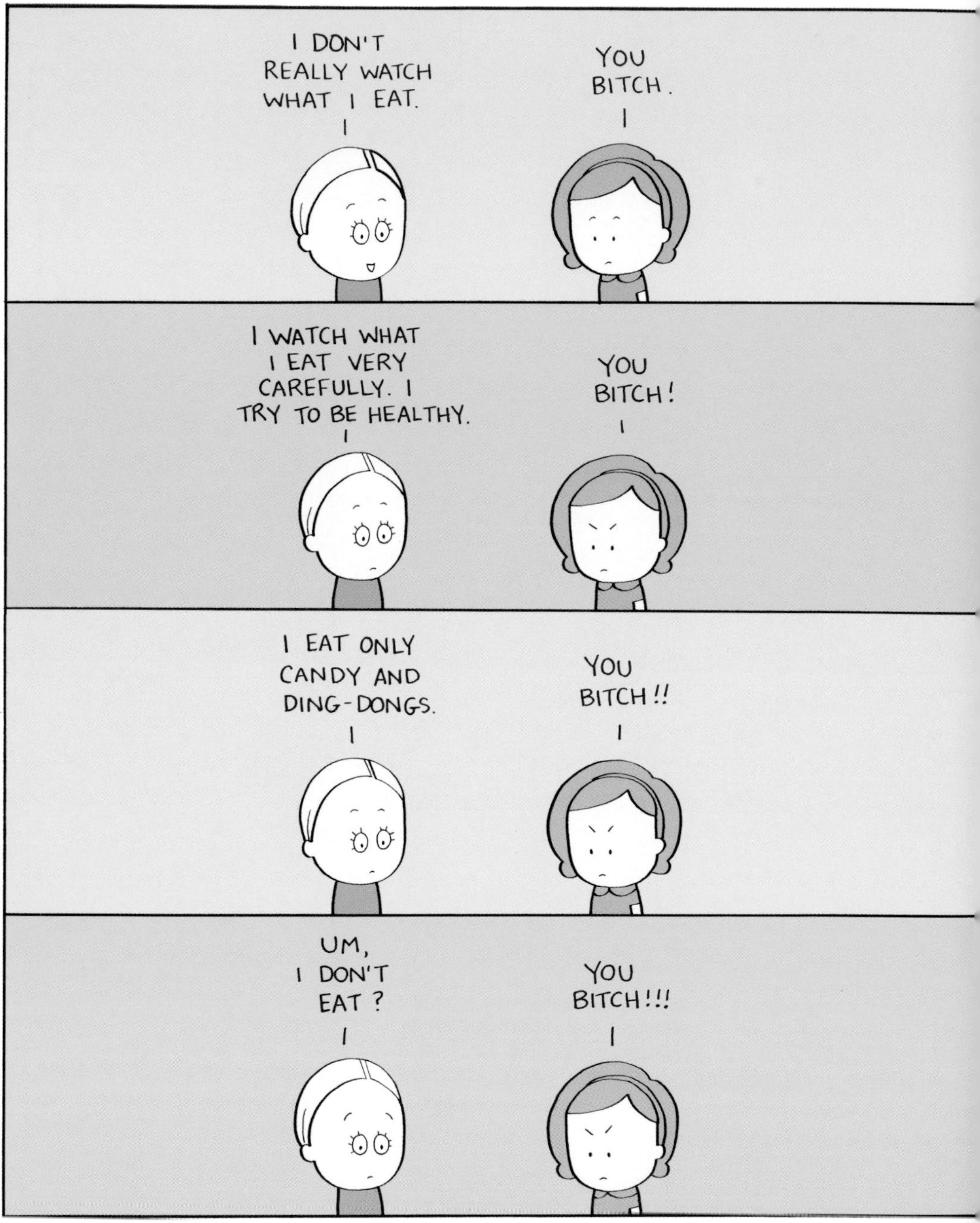
I DON'T REALLY WATCH WHAT I EAT.
YOU BITCH.
I WATCH WHAT I EAT VERY CAREFULLY. I TRY TO BE HEALTHY.
YOU BITCH!
I EAT ONLY CANDY AND DING-DONGS.
YOU BITCH!!
UM, I DON'T EAT?
YOU BITCH!!!

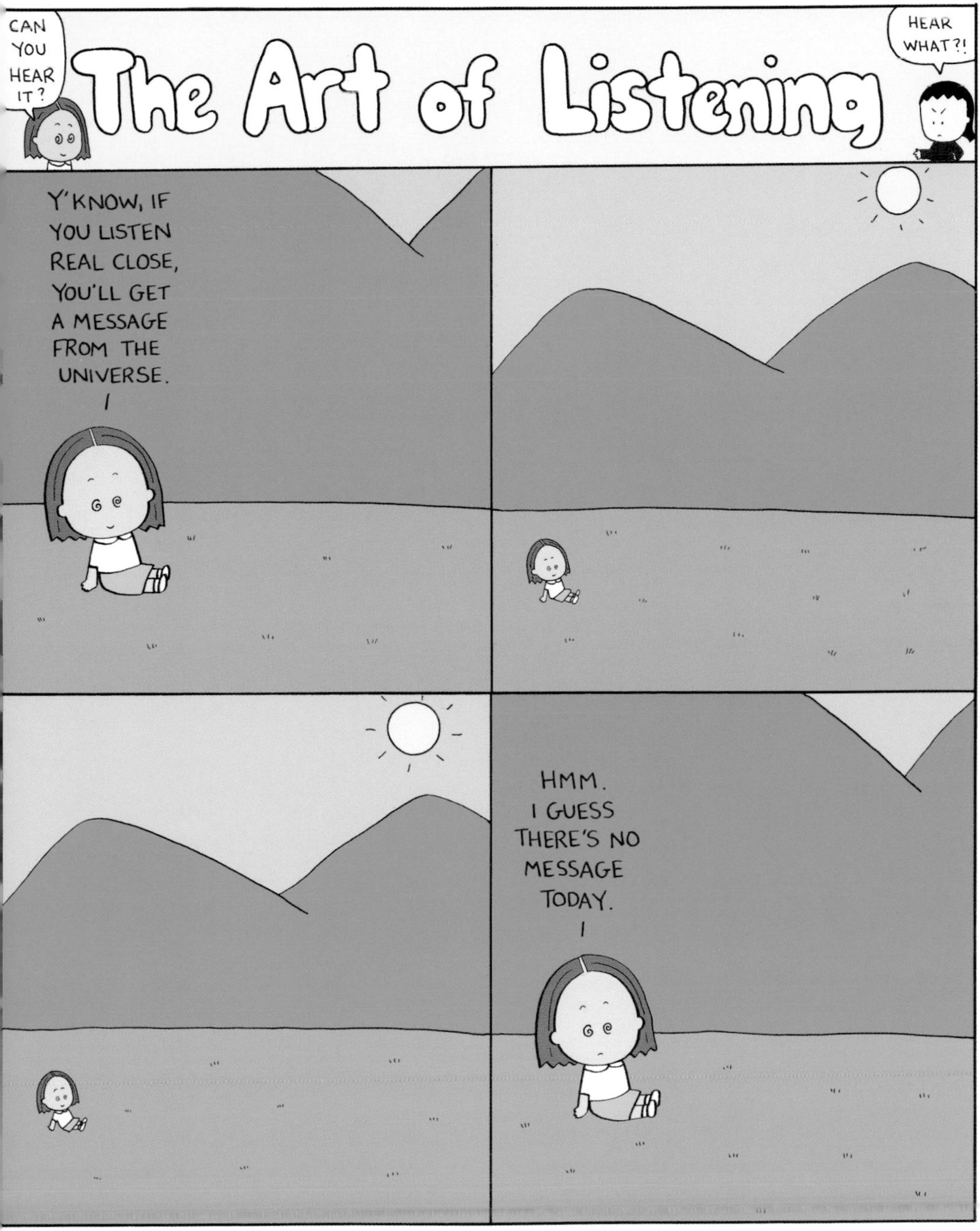
CAN YOU HEAR IT?
The Art of Listening
HEAR WHAT?!
Y'KNOW, IF YOU LISTEN REAL CLOSE, YOU'LL GET A MESSAGE FROM THE UNIVERSE.
HMM. I GUESS THERE'S NO MESSAGE TODAY.

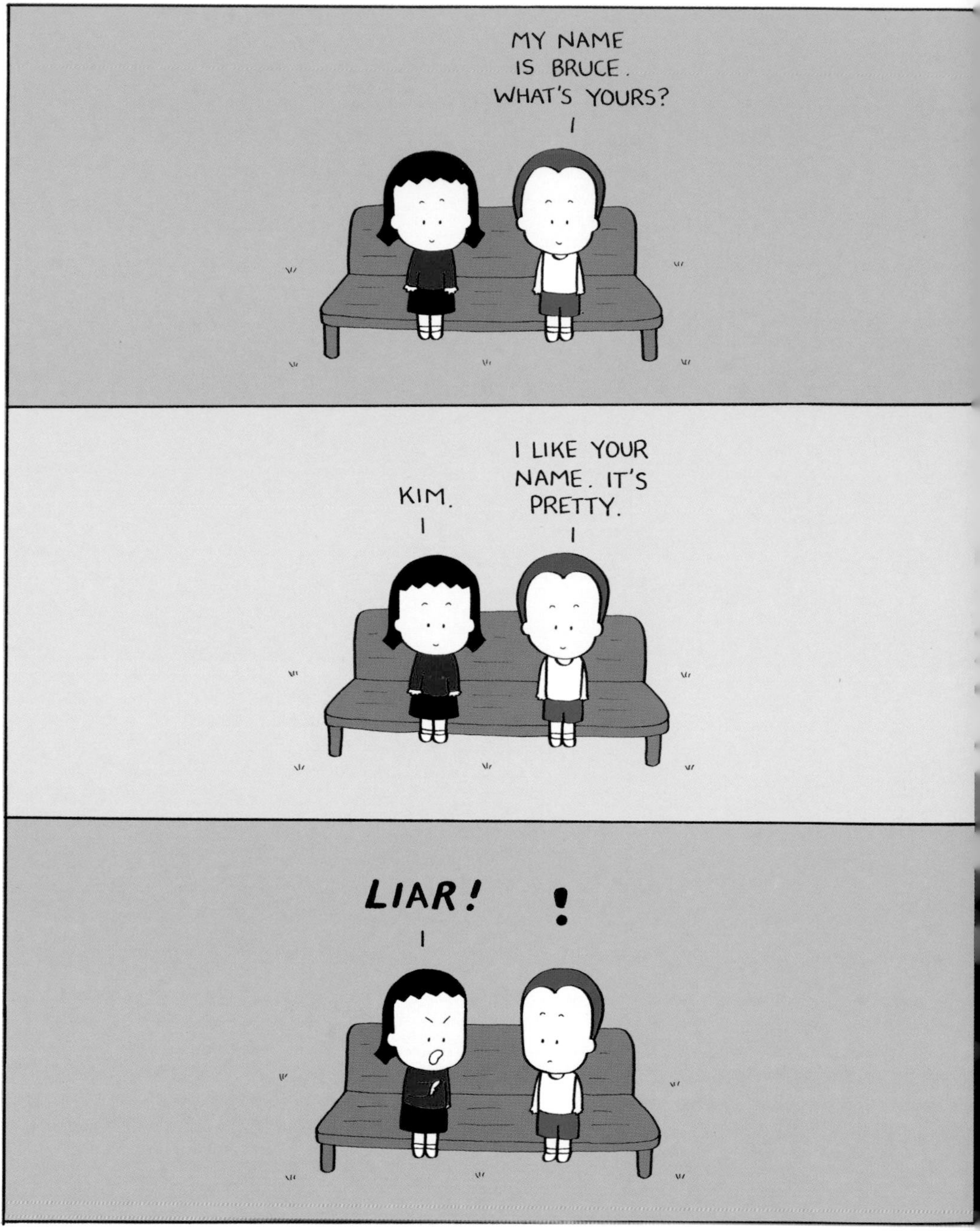
MY NAME IS BRUCE. WHAT'S YOURS?
KIM.
I LIKE YOUR NAME. IT'S PRETTY.
LIAR!
!

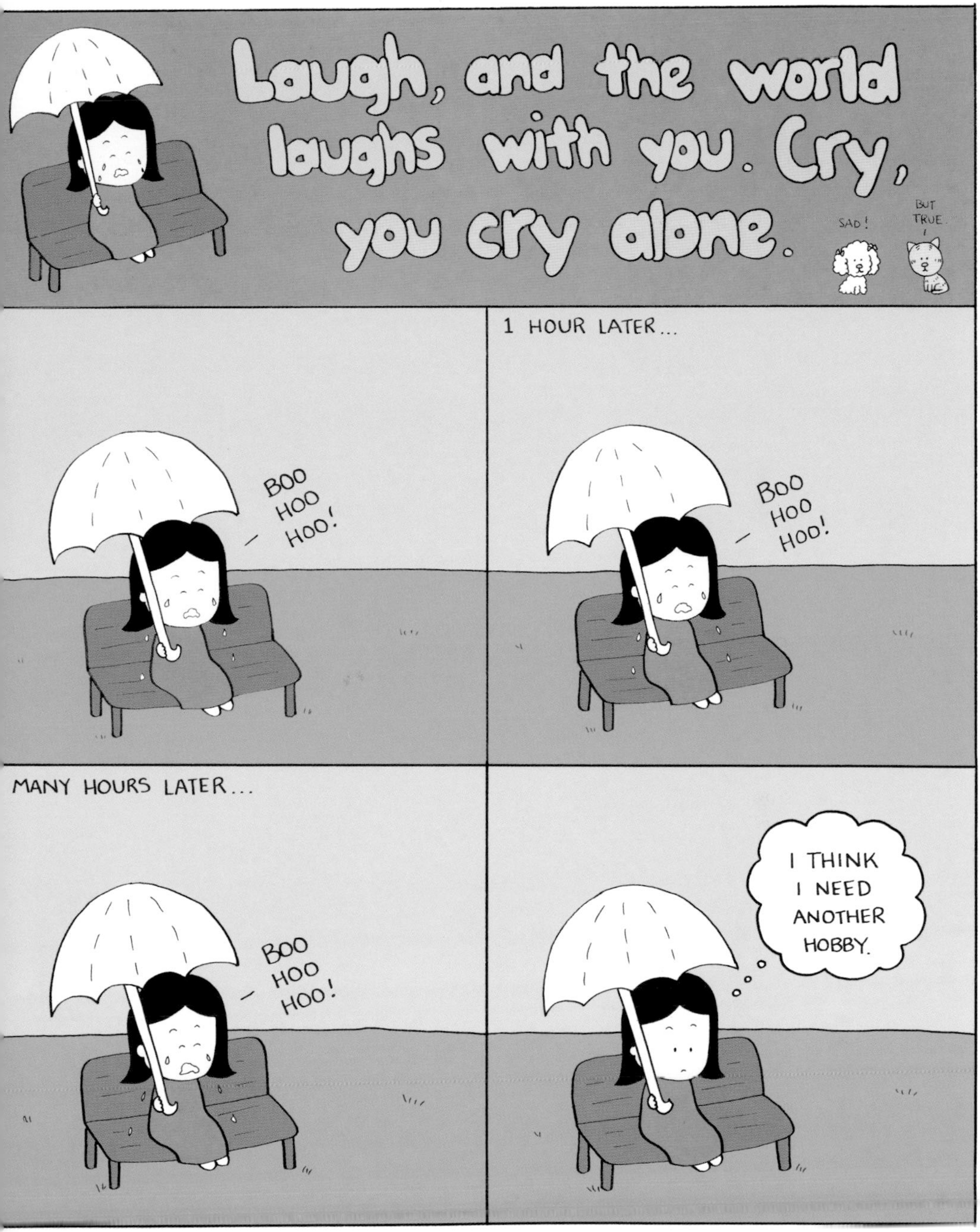
Laugh, and the world laughs with you. Cry, you cry alone.
SAD!
BUT TRUE.
BOO HOO HOO!
1 HOUR LATER...
BOO HOO HOO!
MANY HOURS LATER...
BOO HOO HOO!
I THINK I NEED ANOTHER HOBBY.

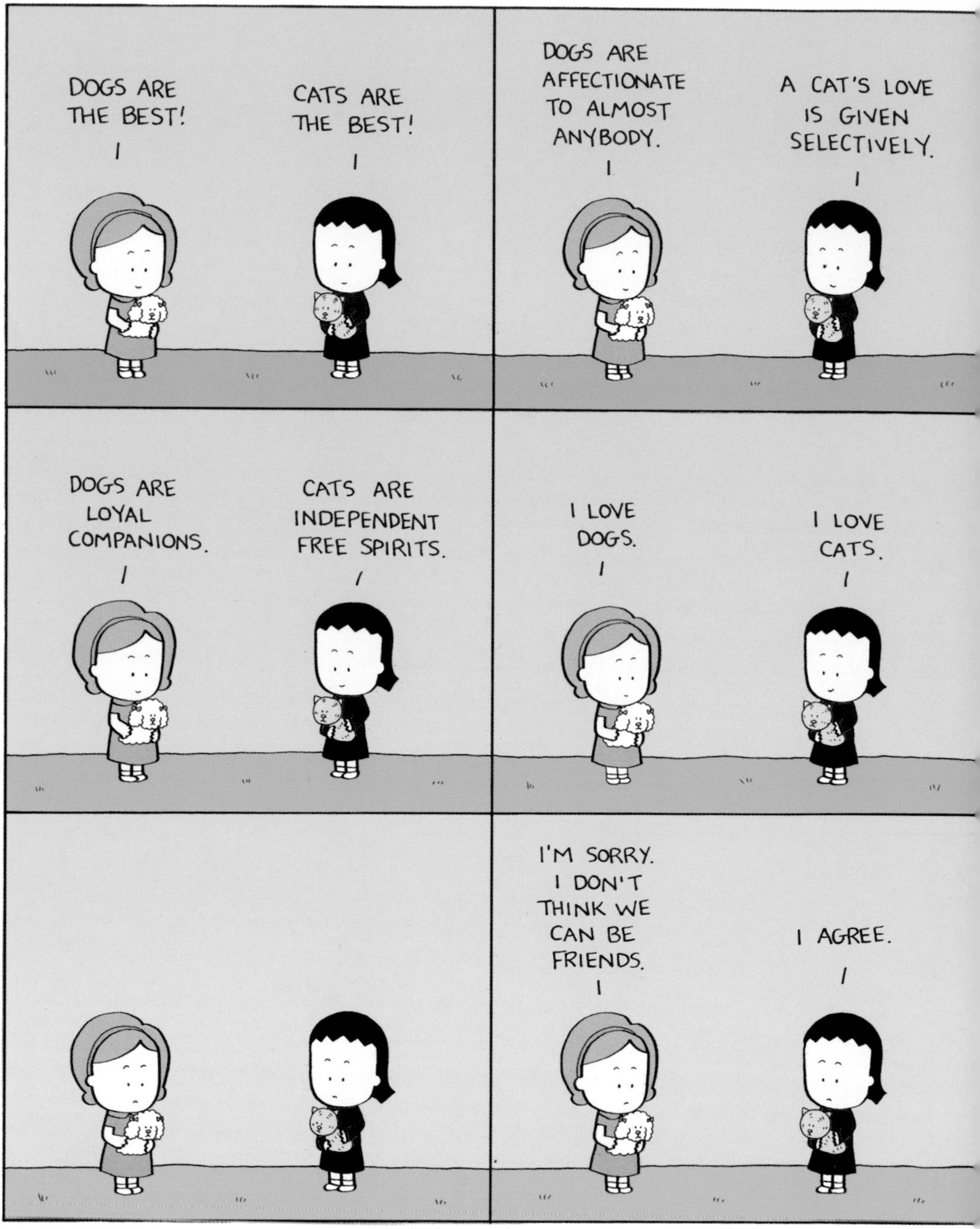

DOGS ARE THE BEST!
CATS ARE THE BEST!
DOGS ARE AFFECTIONATE TO ALMOST ANYBODY.
A CAT'S LOVE IS GIVEN SELECTIVELY.
DOGS ARE LOYAL COMPANIONS.
CATS ARE INDEPENDENT FREE SPIRITS.
I LOVE DOGS.
I LOVE CATS.
I'M SORRY. I DON'T THINK WE CAN BE FRIENDS.
I AGREE.

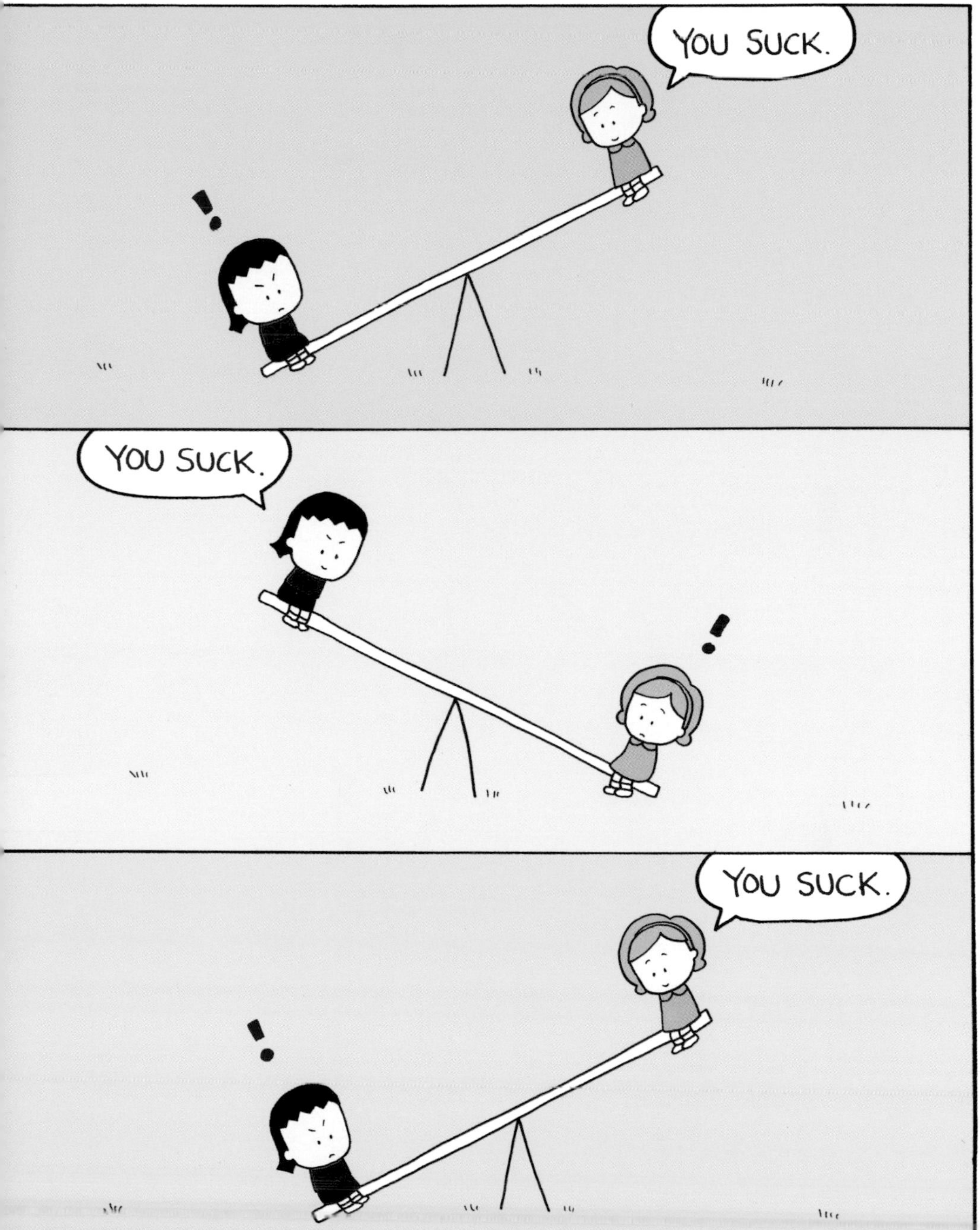
YOU SUCK.
YOU SUCK.
YOU SUCK.

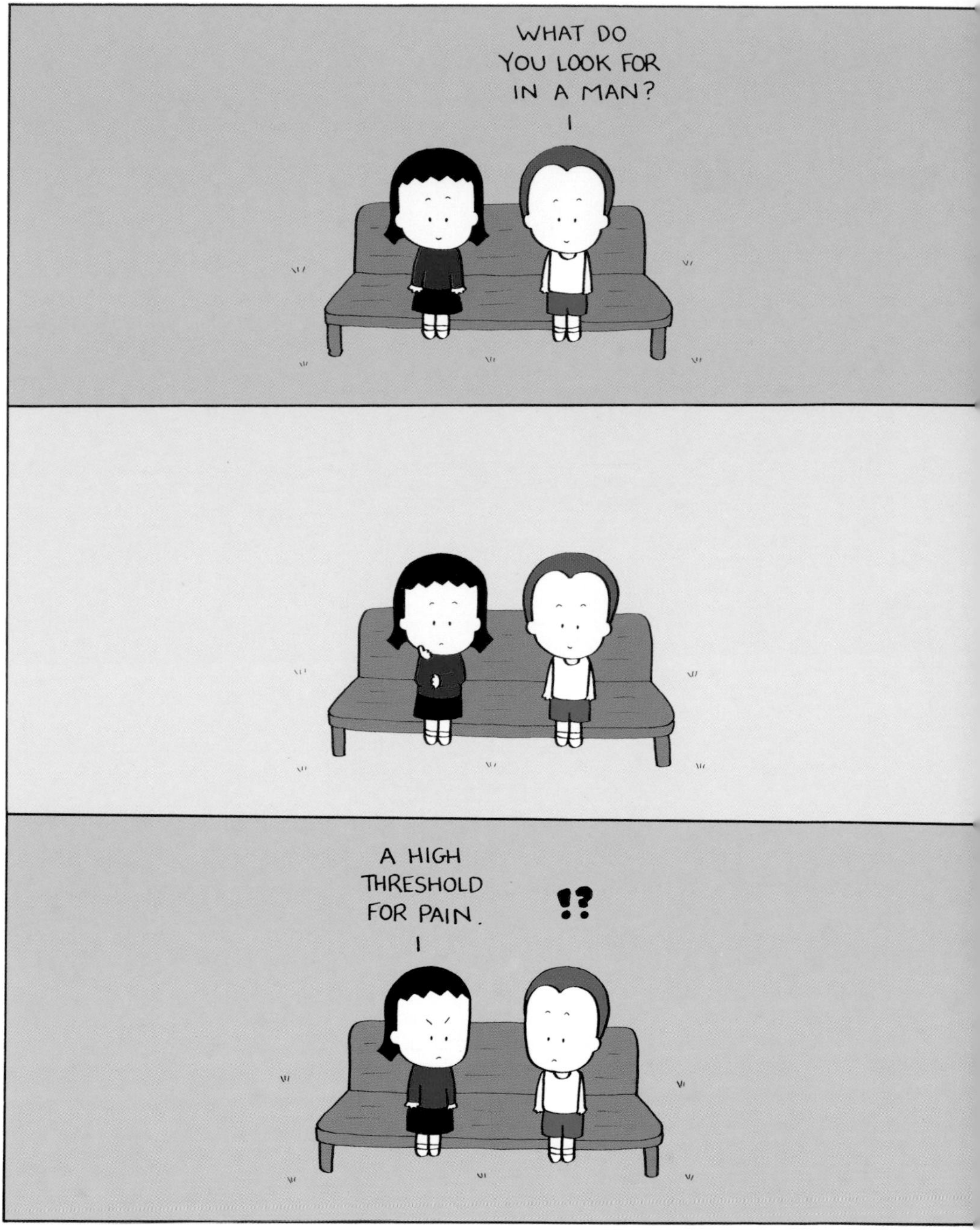
WHAT DO YOU LOOK FOR IN A MAN?
A HIGH THRESHOLD FOR PAIN.
!?

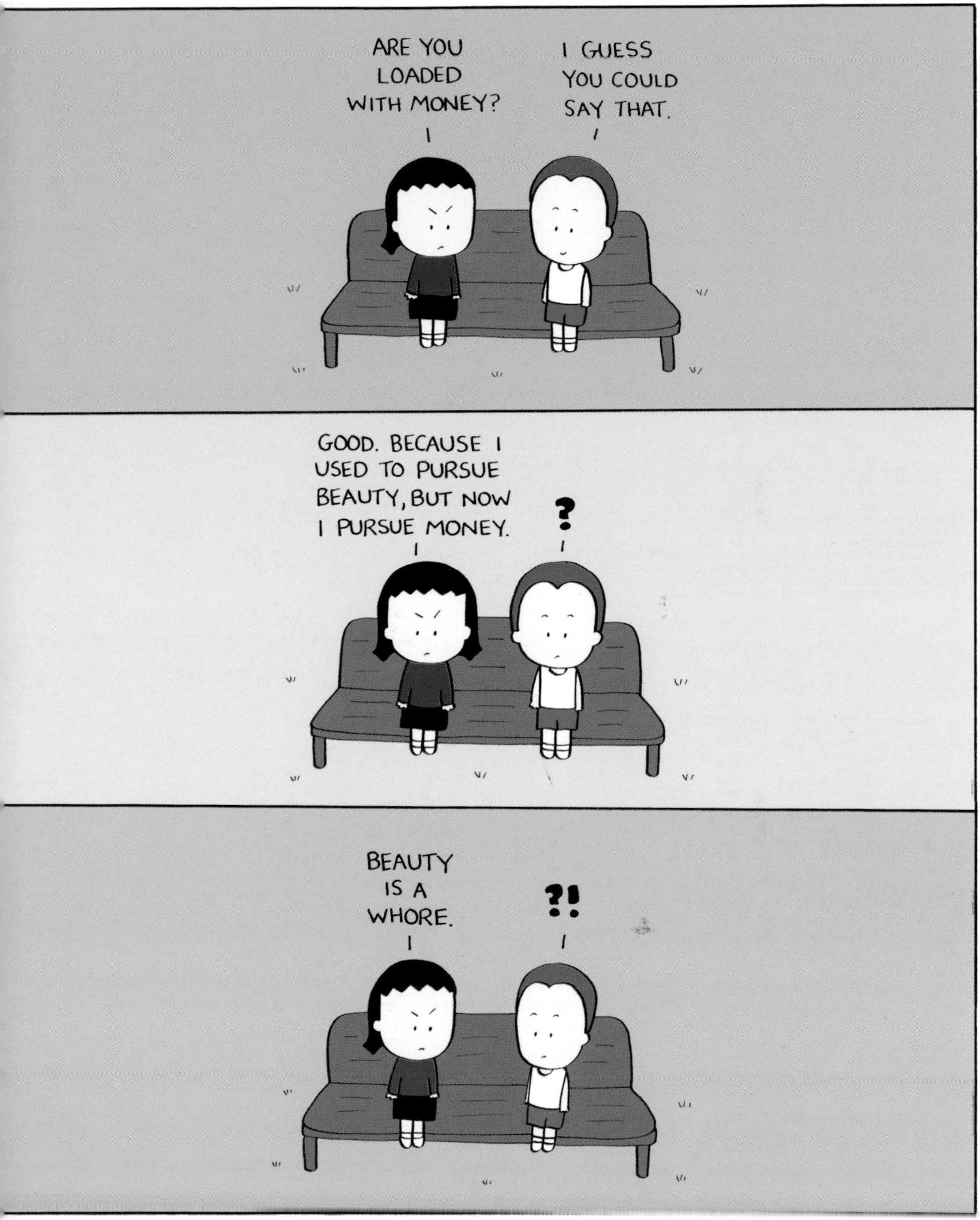
ARE YOU LOADED WITH MONEY?
I GUESS YOU COULD SAY THAT.
GOOD. BECAUSE I USED TO PURSUE BEAUTY, BUT NOW I PURSUE MONEY.
?
BEAUTY IS A WHORE.
?!

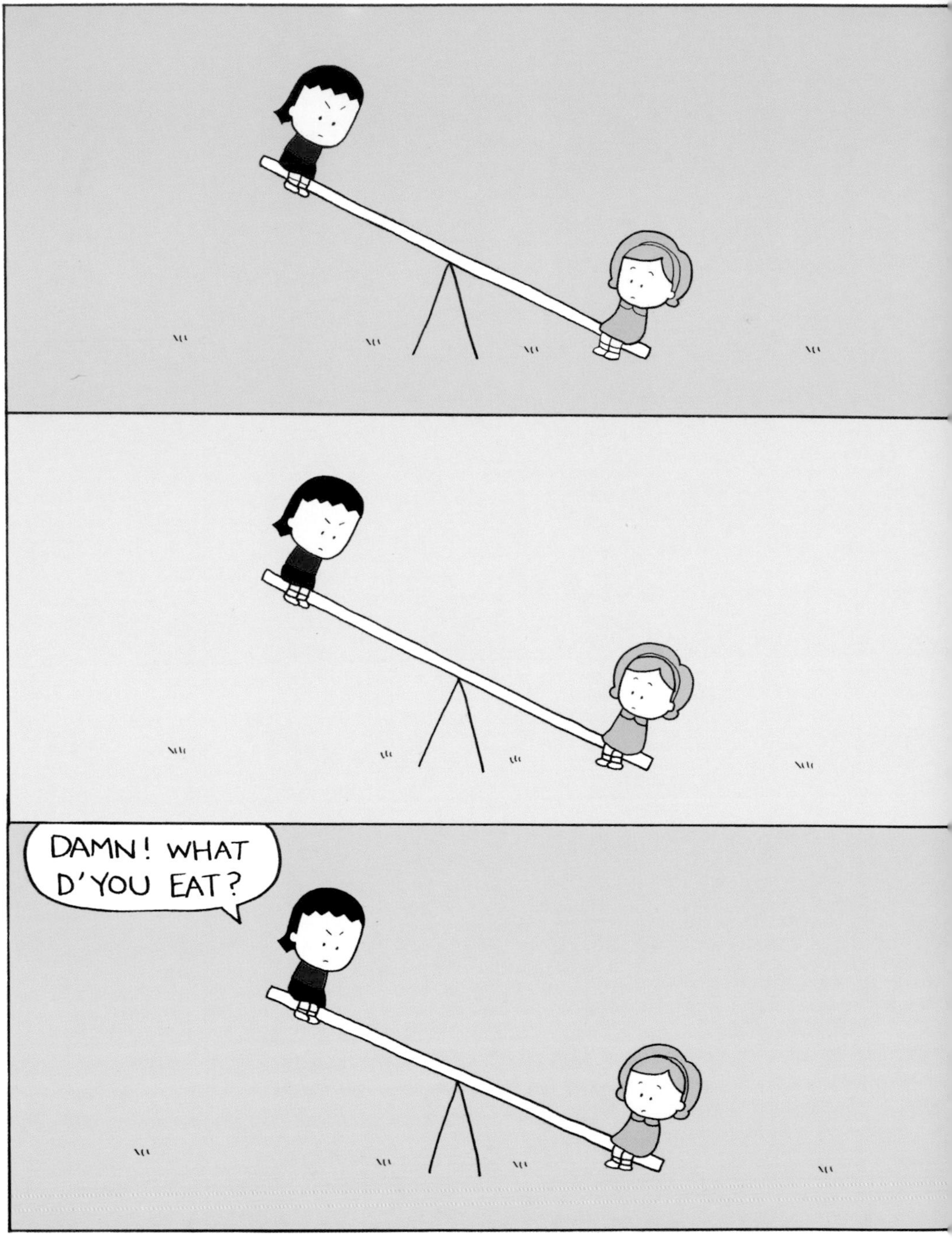
DAMN! WHAT D'YOU EAT?

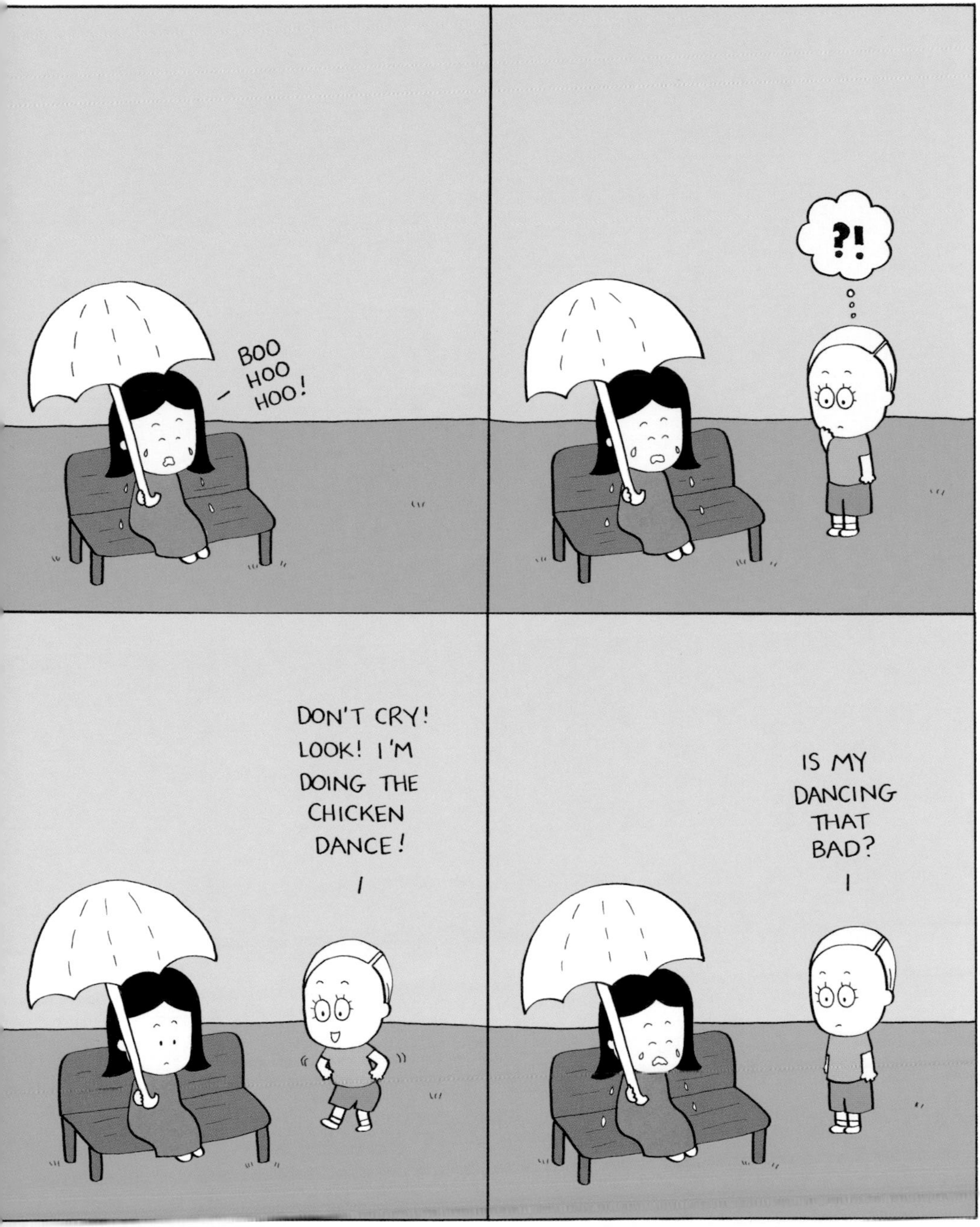
BOO HOO HOO!
?!
DON'T CRY! LOOK! I'M DOING THE CHICKEN DANCE!
IS MY DANCING THAT BAD?

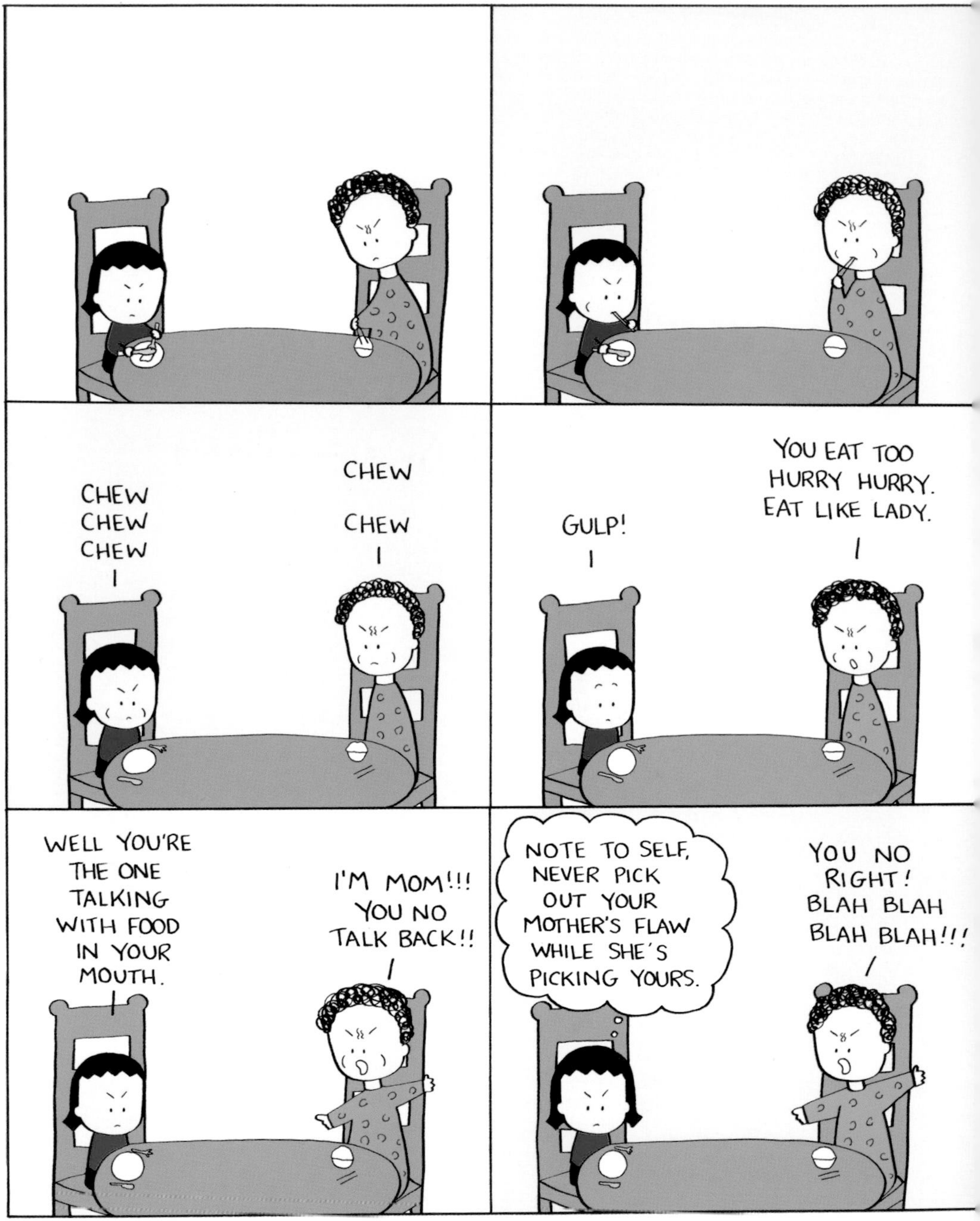
CHEW
CHEW
CHEW
CHEW
CHEW
GULP!
YOU EAT TOO HURRY HURRY. EAT LIKE LADY.
WELL YOU'RE THE ONE TALKING WITH FOOD IN YOUR MOUTH.
I'M MOM!!! YOU NO TALK BACK!!
NOTE TO SELF, NEVER PICK OUT YOUR MOTHER'S FLAW WHILE SHE'S PICKING YOURS.
YOU NO RIGHT! BLAH BLAH BLAH BLAH!!!

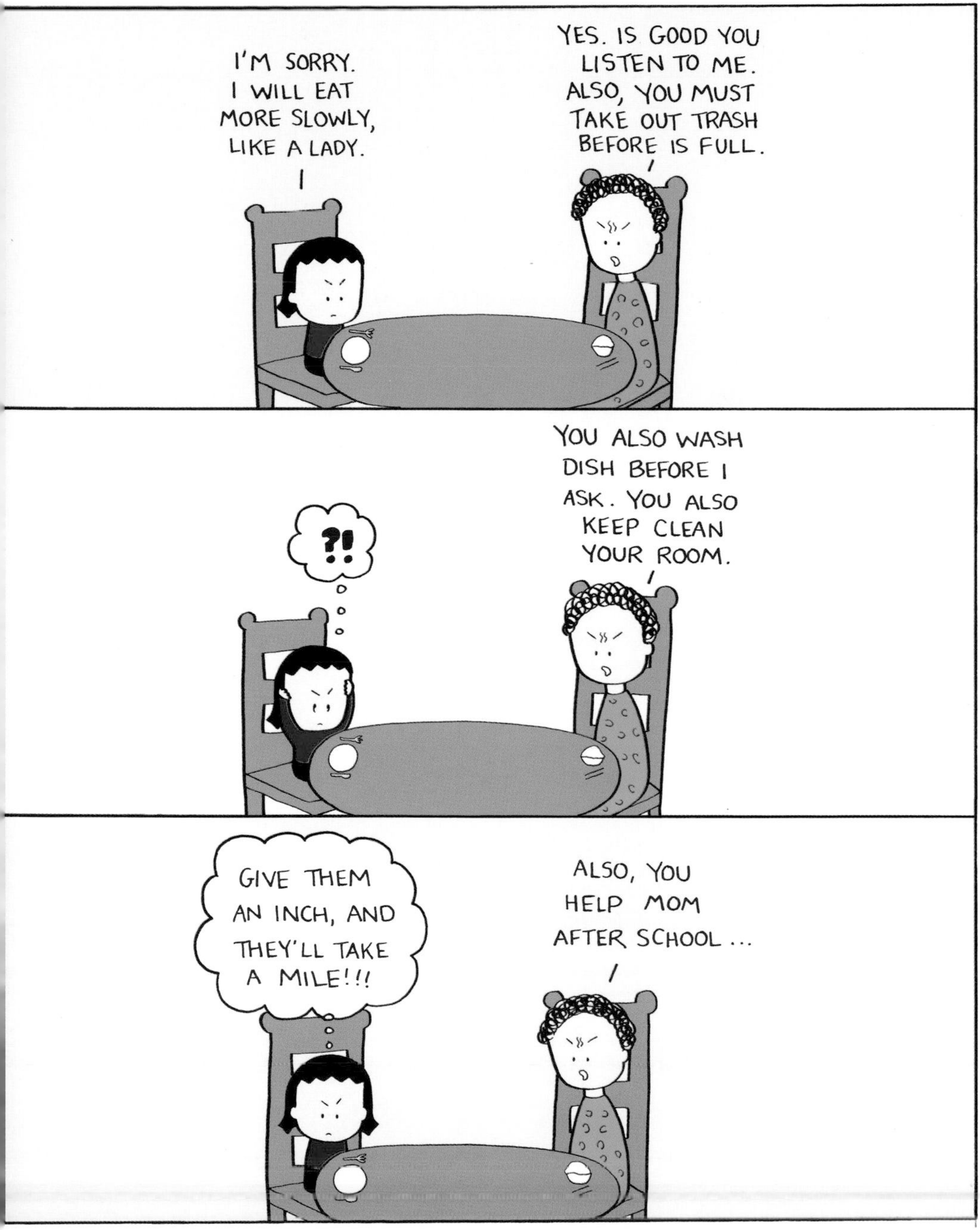
I'M SORRY. I WILL EAT MORE SLOWLY, LIKE A LADY.
YES. IS GOOD YOU LISTEN TO ME. ALSO, YOU MUST TAKE OUT TRASH BEFORE IS FULL.
?!
YOU ALSO WASH DISH BEFORE I ASK. YOU ALSO KEEP CLEAN YOUR ROOM.
GIVE THEM AN INCH, AND THEY'LL TAKE A MILE!!!
ALSO, YOU HELP MOM AFTER SCHOOL...

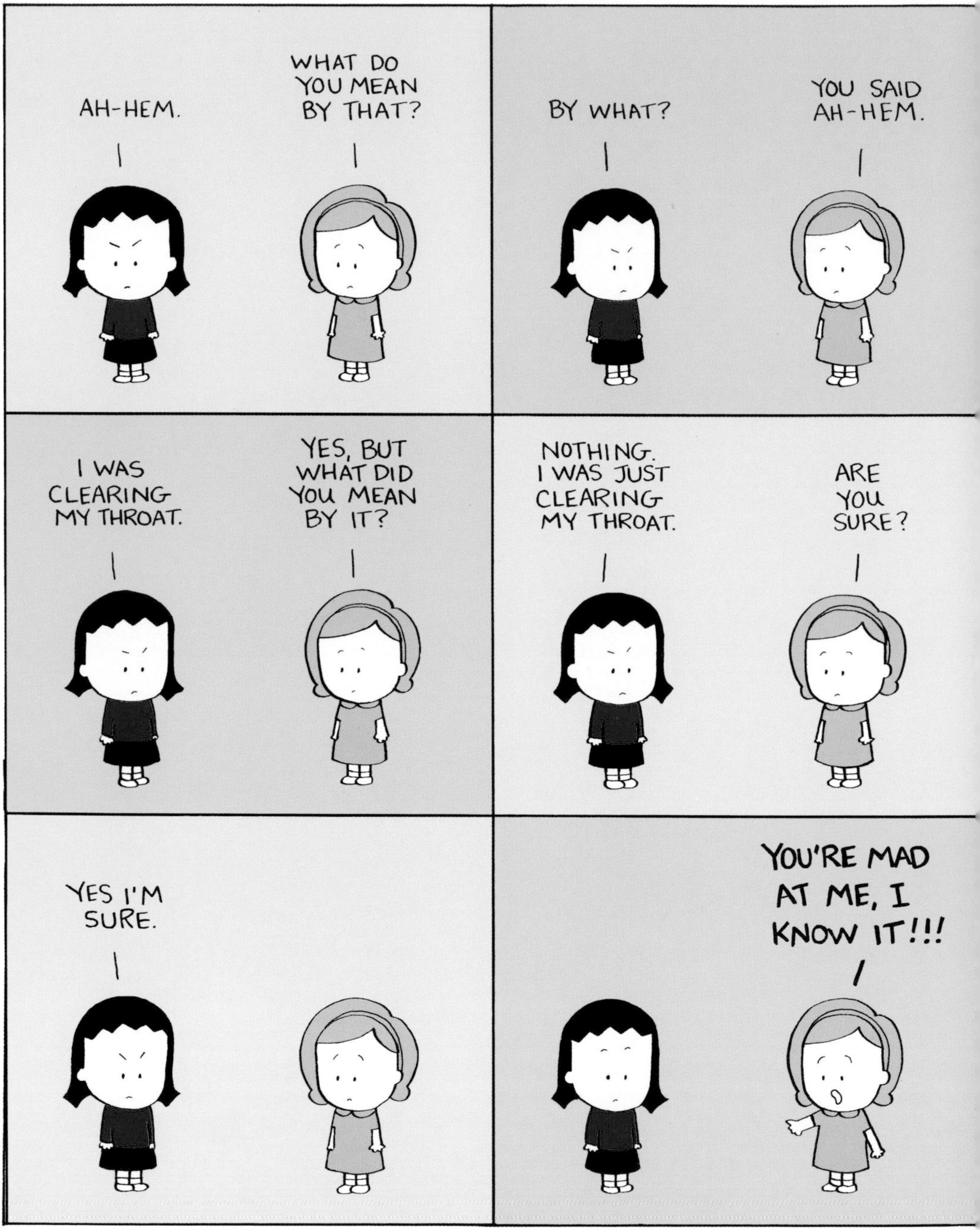
AH-HEM.
WHAT DO YOU MEAN BY THAT?
BY WHAT?
YOU SAID AH-HEM.
I WAS CLEARING MY THROAT.
YES, BUT WHAT DID YOU MEAN BY IT?
NOTHING. I WAS JUST CLEARING MY THROAT.
ARE YOU SURE?
YES I'M SURE.
YOU'RE MAD AT ME, I KNOW IT!!!

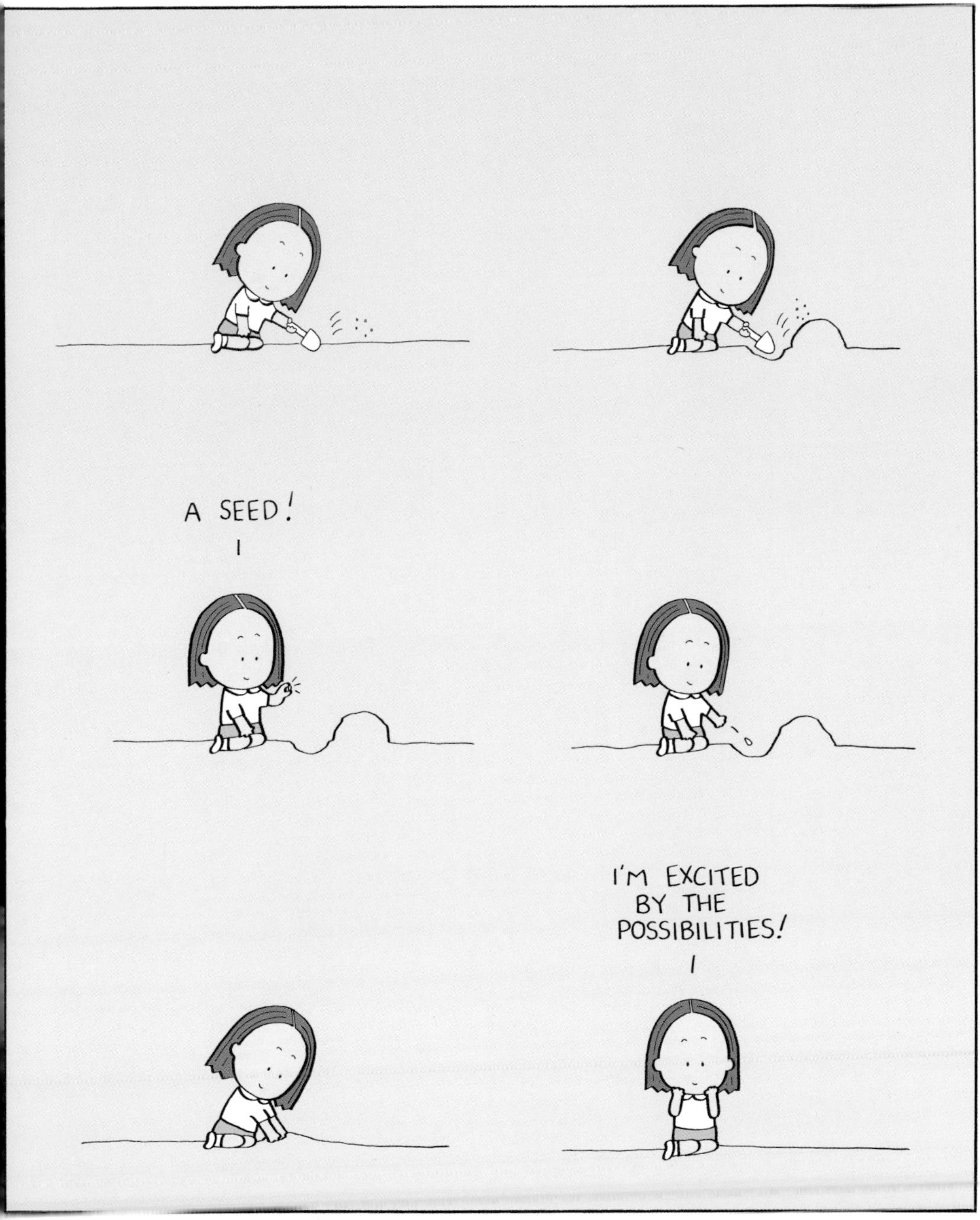
A SEED!
I'M EXCITED BY THE POSSIBILITIES!

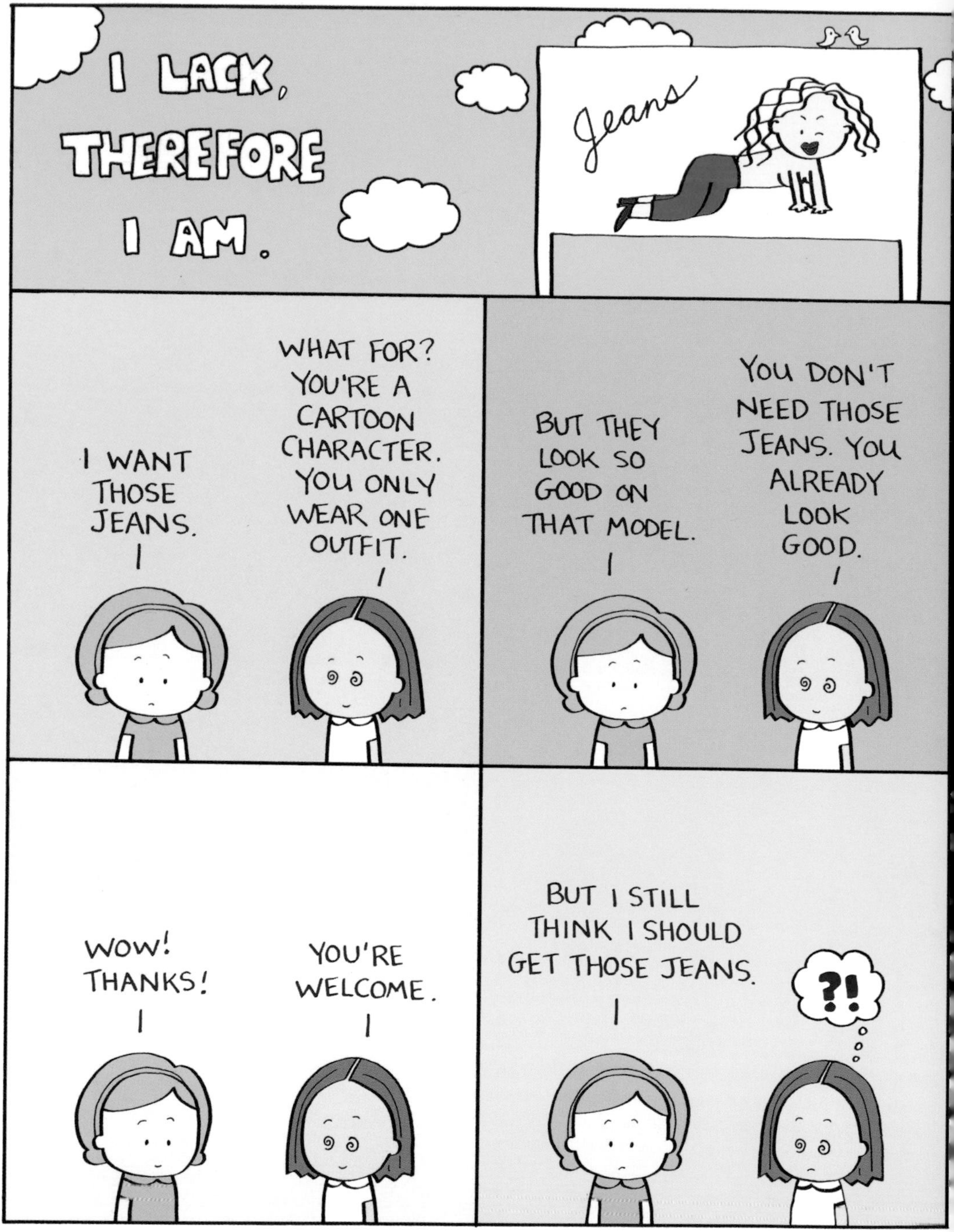
I LACK, THEREFORE I AM.
Jeans
I WANT THOSE JEANS.
WHAT FOR? YOU'RE A CARTOON CHARACTER. YOU ONLY WEAR ONE OUTFIT.
BUT THEY LOOK SO GOOD ON THAT MODEL.
YOU DON'T NEED THOSE JEANS. YOU ALREADY LOOK GOOD.
WOW! THANKS!
YOU'RE WELCOME.
BUT I STILL THINK I SHOULD GET THOSE JEANS.
?!

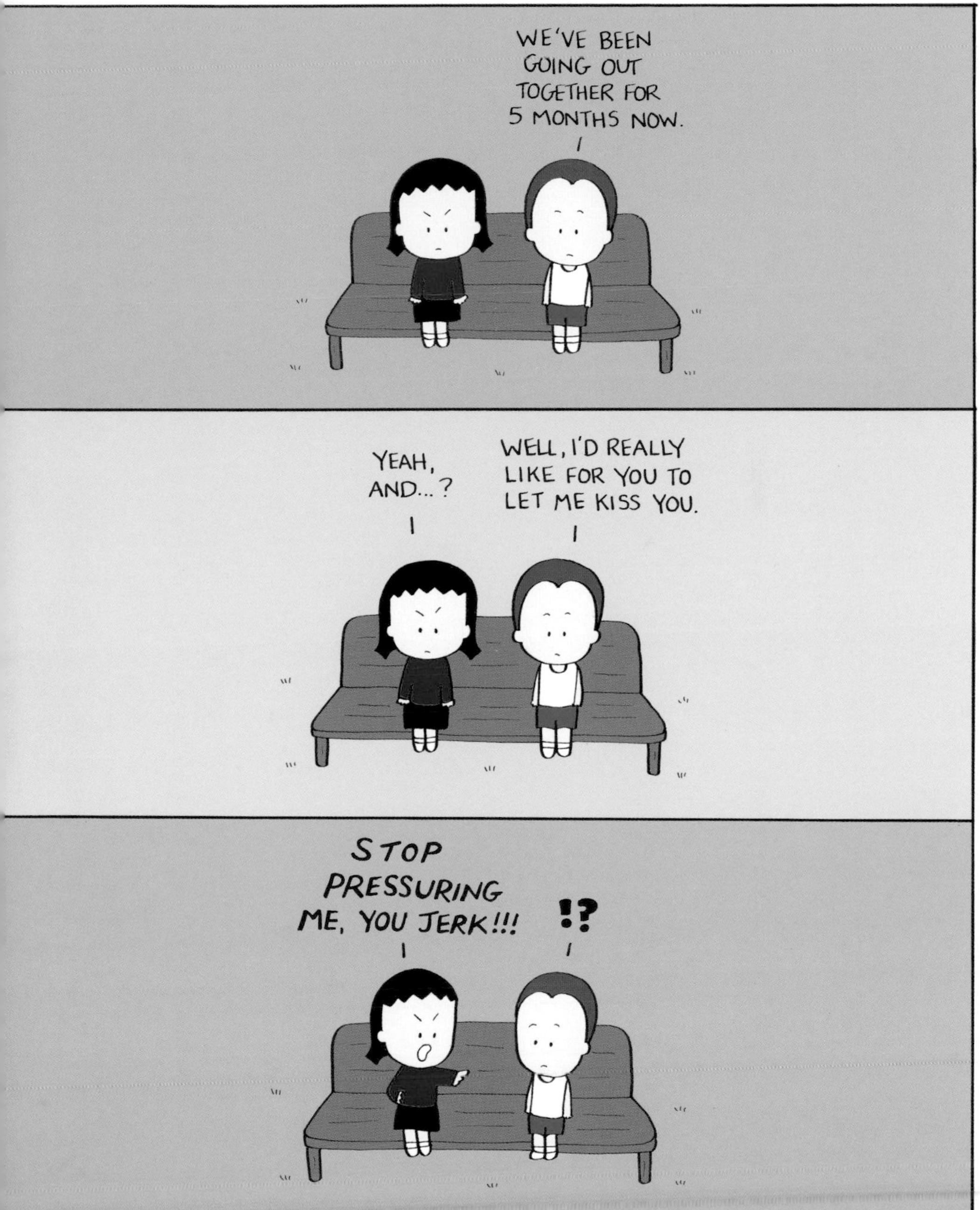
WE'VE BEEN GOING OUT TOGETHER FOR 5 MONTHS NOW.
YEAH, AND...?
WELL, I'D REALLY LIKE FOR YOU TO LET ME KISS YOU.
STOP PRESSURING ME, YOU JERK!!!
!?

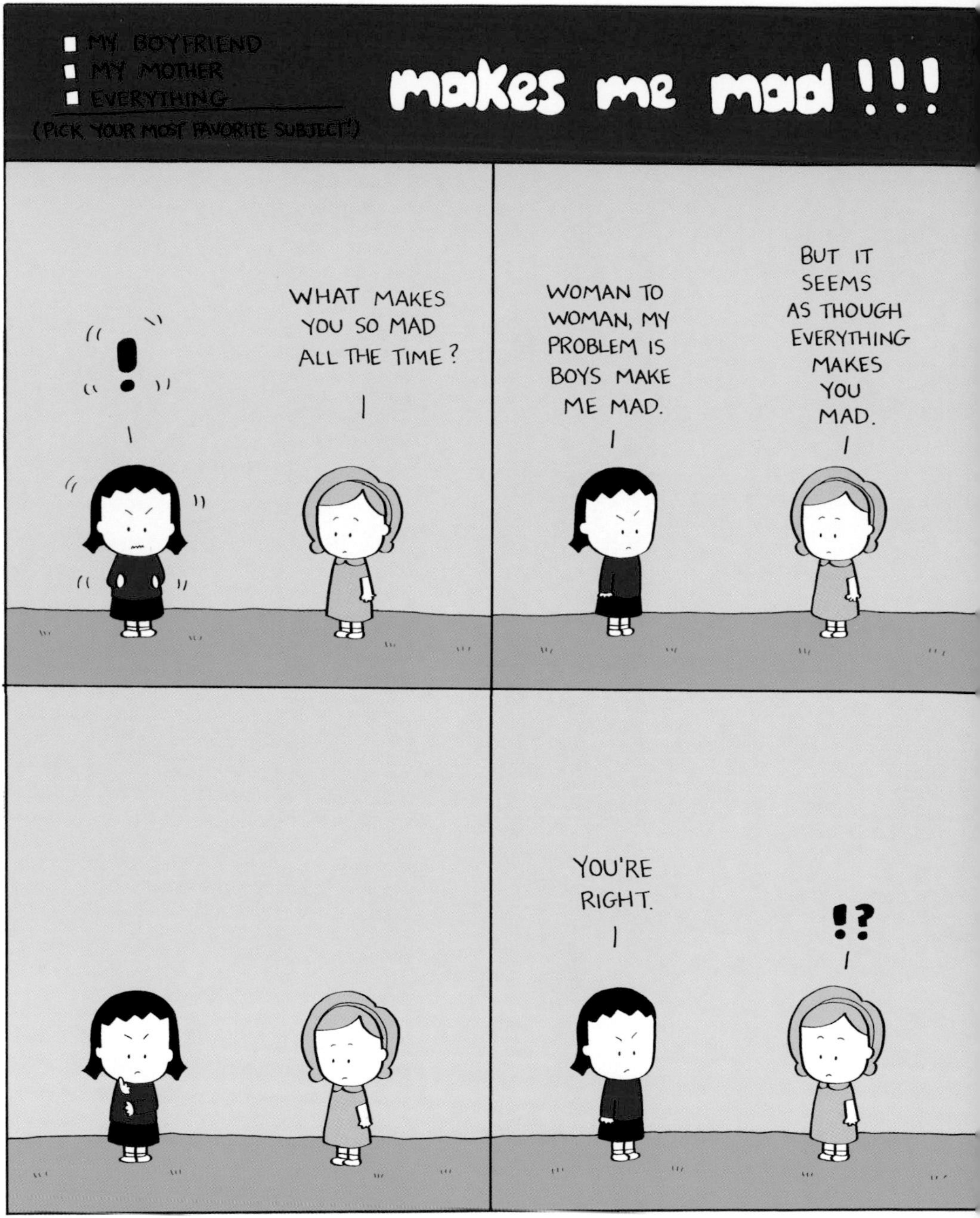

MY BOYFRIEND
MY MOTHER
EVERYTHING
(PICK YOUR MOST FAVORITE SUBJECT!)
makes me mad !!!
WHAT MAKES YOU SO MAD ALL THE TIME?
!
WOMAN TO WOMAN, MY PROBLEM IS BOYS MAKE ME MAD.
BUT IT SEEMS AS THOUGH EVERYTHING MAKES YOU MAD.
YOU'RE RIGHT.
!?

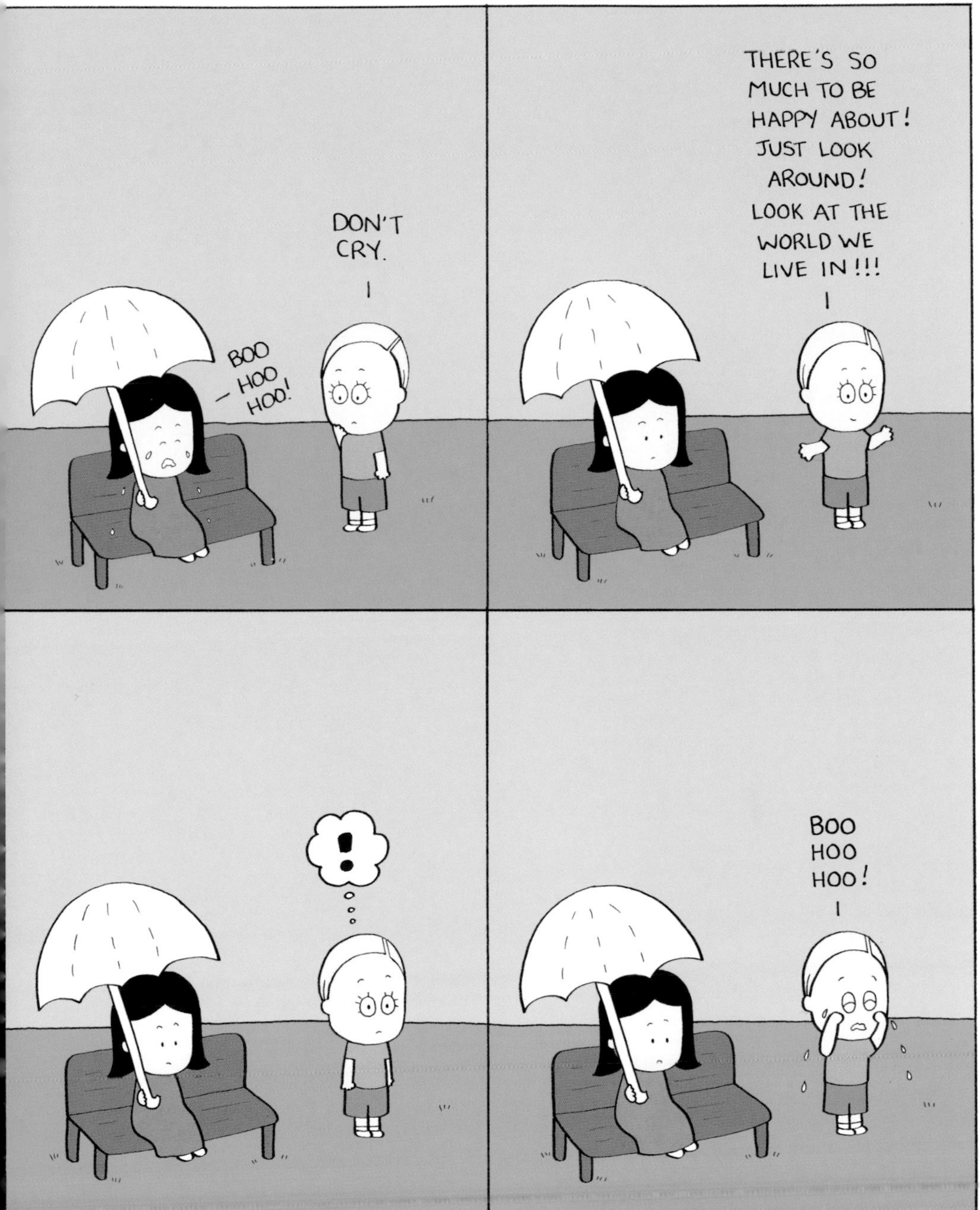
DON'T CRY.
BOO - HOO HOO!
THERE'S SO MUCH TO BE HAPPY ABOUT! JUST LOOK AROUND! LOOK AT THE WORLD WE LIVE IN!!!
!
BOO HOO HOO!

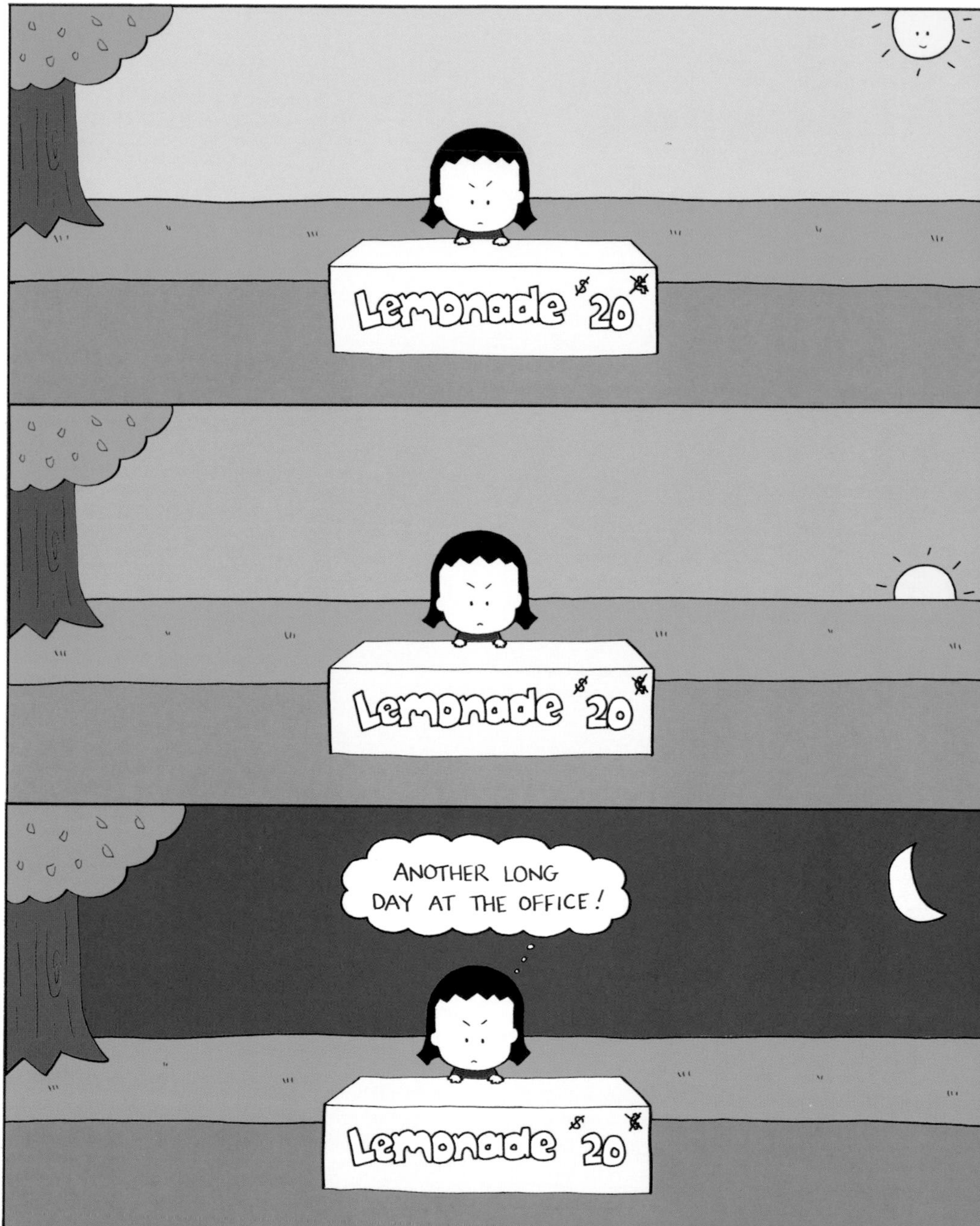

Lemonade 20
Lemonade 20
ANOTHER LONG DAY AT THE OFFICE!
Lemonade 20

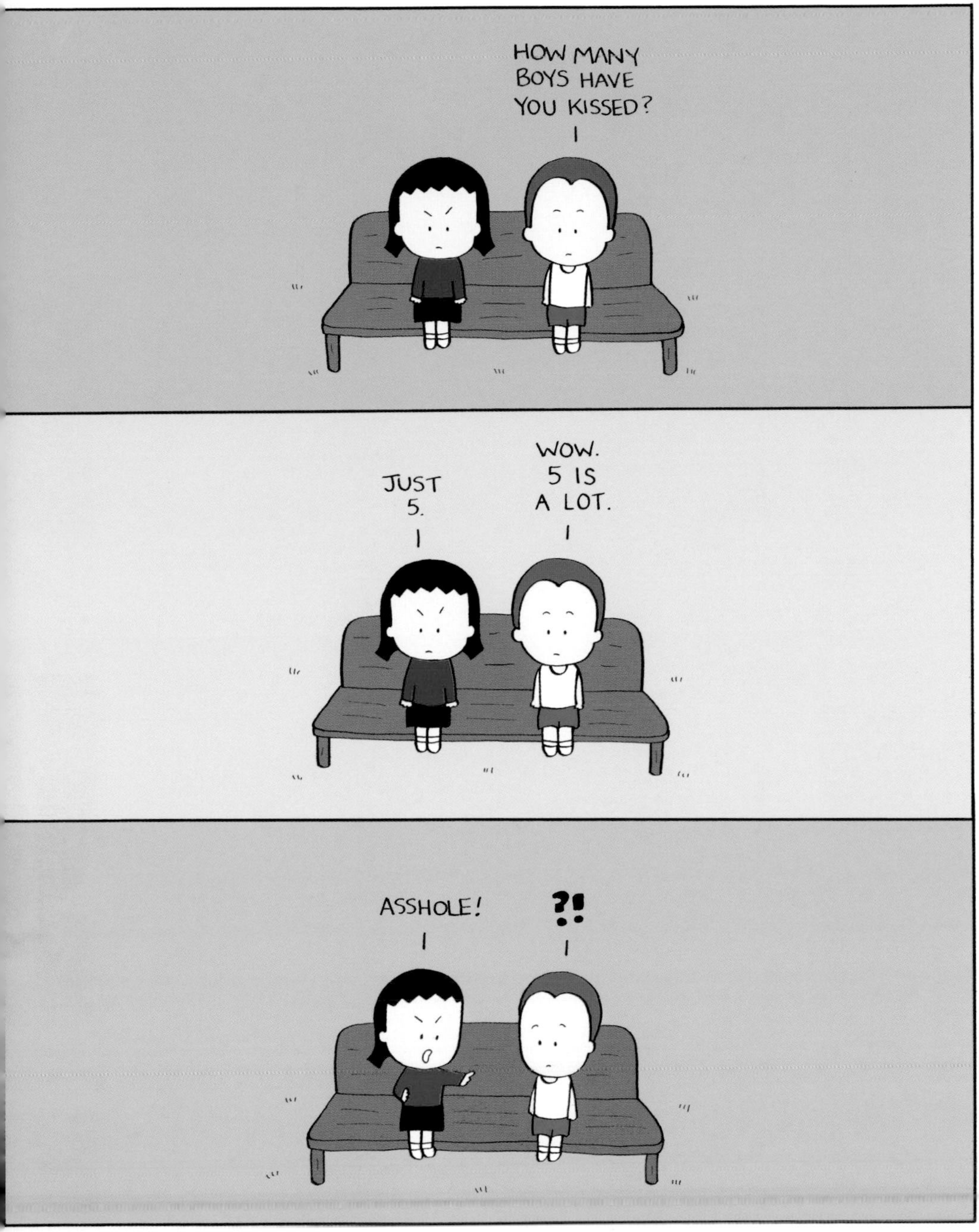
HOW MANY BOYS HAVE YOU KISSED?
JUST 5.
WOW. 5 IS A LOT.
ASSHOLE!
?!

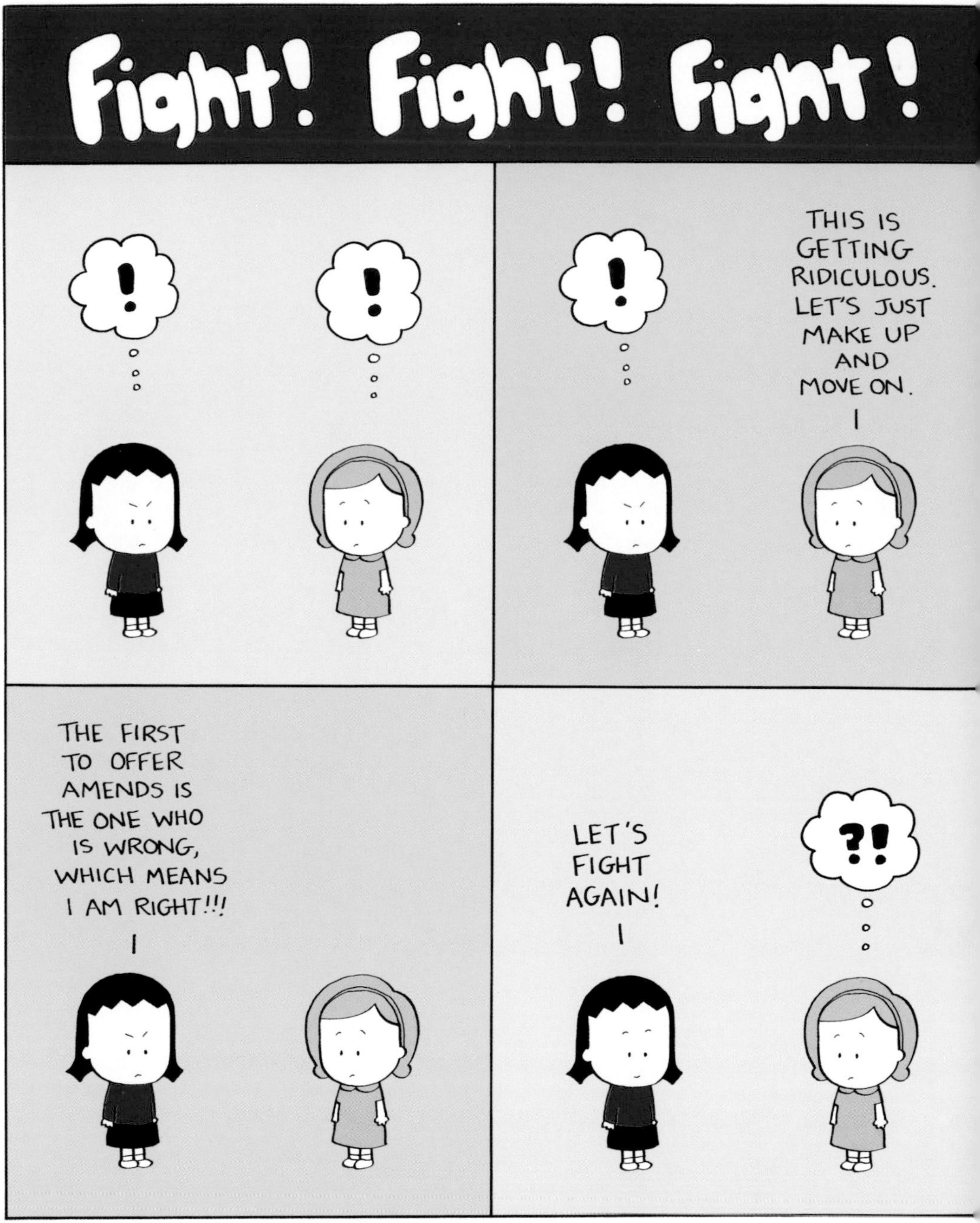
Fight! Fight! Fight!
!
!
!
THIS IS GETTING RIDICULOUS. LET'S JUST MAKE UP AND MOVE ON.
THE FIRST TO OFFER AMENDS IS THE ONE WHO IS WRONG, WHICH MEANS I AM RIGHT!!!
LET'S FIGHT AGAIN!
?!

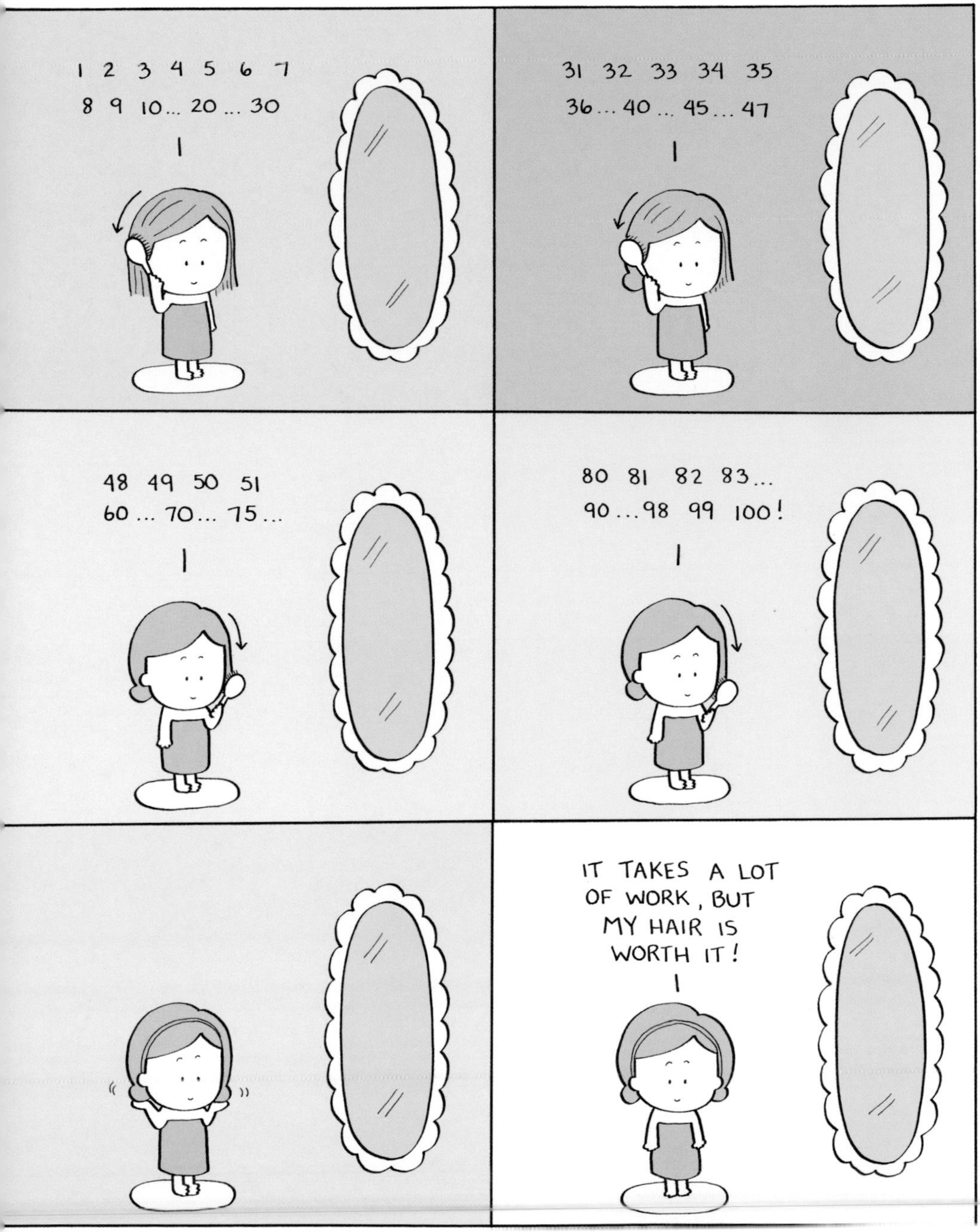
1 2 3 4 5 6 7
8 9 10... 20... 30
31 32 33 34 35
36... 40... 45... 47
48 49 50 51
60... 70... 75...
80 81 82 83...
90...98 99 100!
IT TAKES A LOT OF WORK, BUT MY HAIR IS WORTH IT!

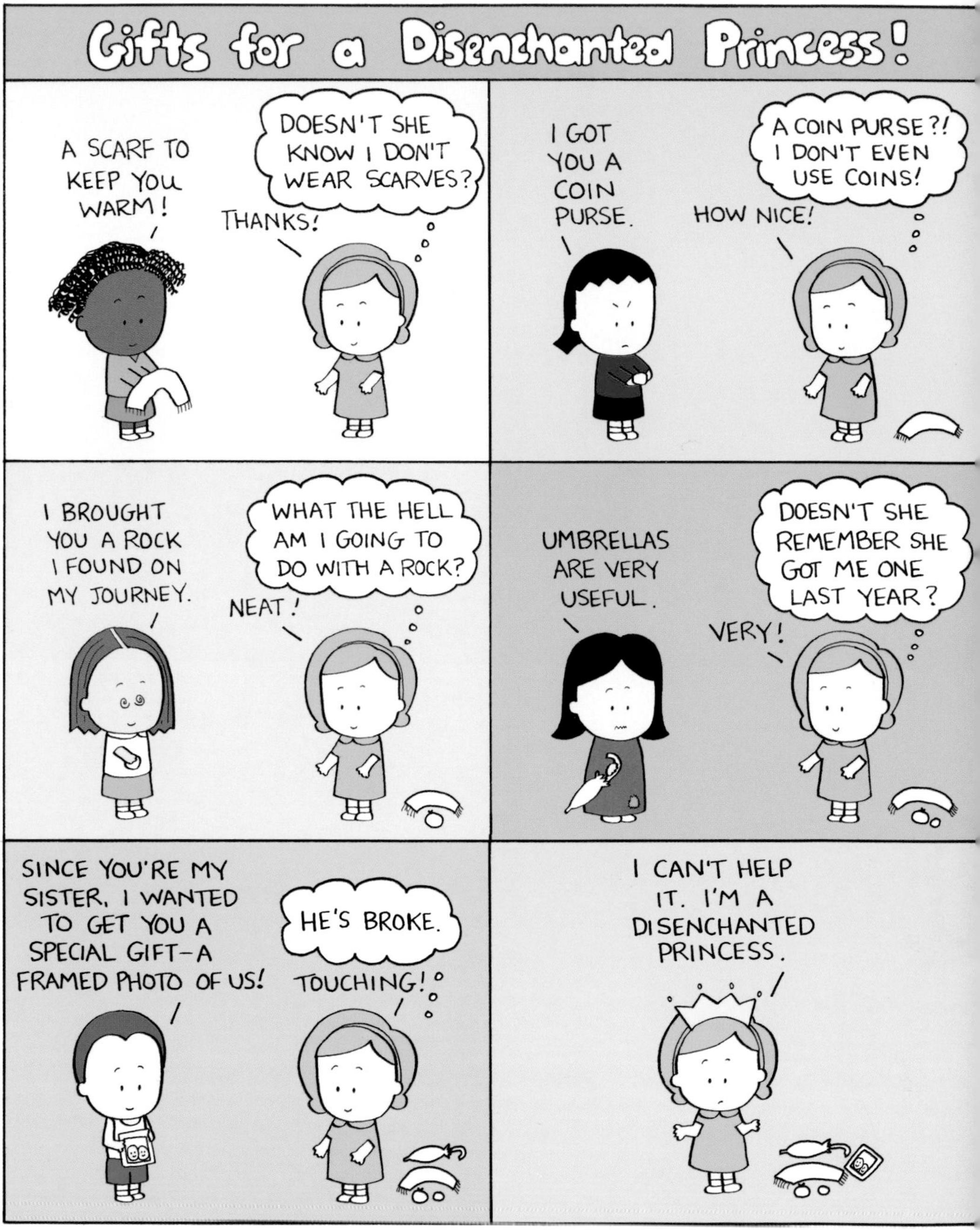
Gifts for a Disenchanted Princess!
A SCARF TO KEEP YOU WARM!
THANKS!
DOESN'T SHE KNOW I DON'T WEAR SCARVES?
I GOT YOU A COIN PURSE.
HOW NICE!
A COIN PURSE?! I DON'T EVEN USE COINS!
I BROUGHT YOU A ROCK I FOUND ON MY JOURNEY.
NEAT!
WHAT THE HELL AM I GOING TO DO WITH A ROCK?
UMBRELLAS ARE VERY USEFUL.
VERY!
DOESN'T SHE REMEMBER SHE GOT ME ONE LAST YEAR?
SINCE YOU'RE MY SISTER, I WANTED TO GET YOU A SPECIAL GIFT—A FRAMED PHOTO OF US!
TOUCHING!
HE'S BROKE.
I CAN'T HELP IT. I'M A DISENCHANTED PRINCESS.

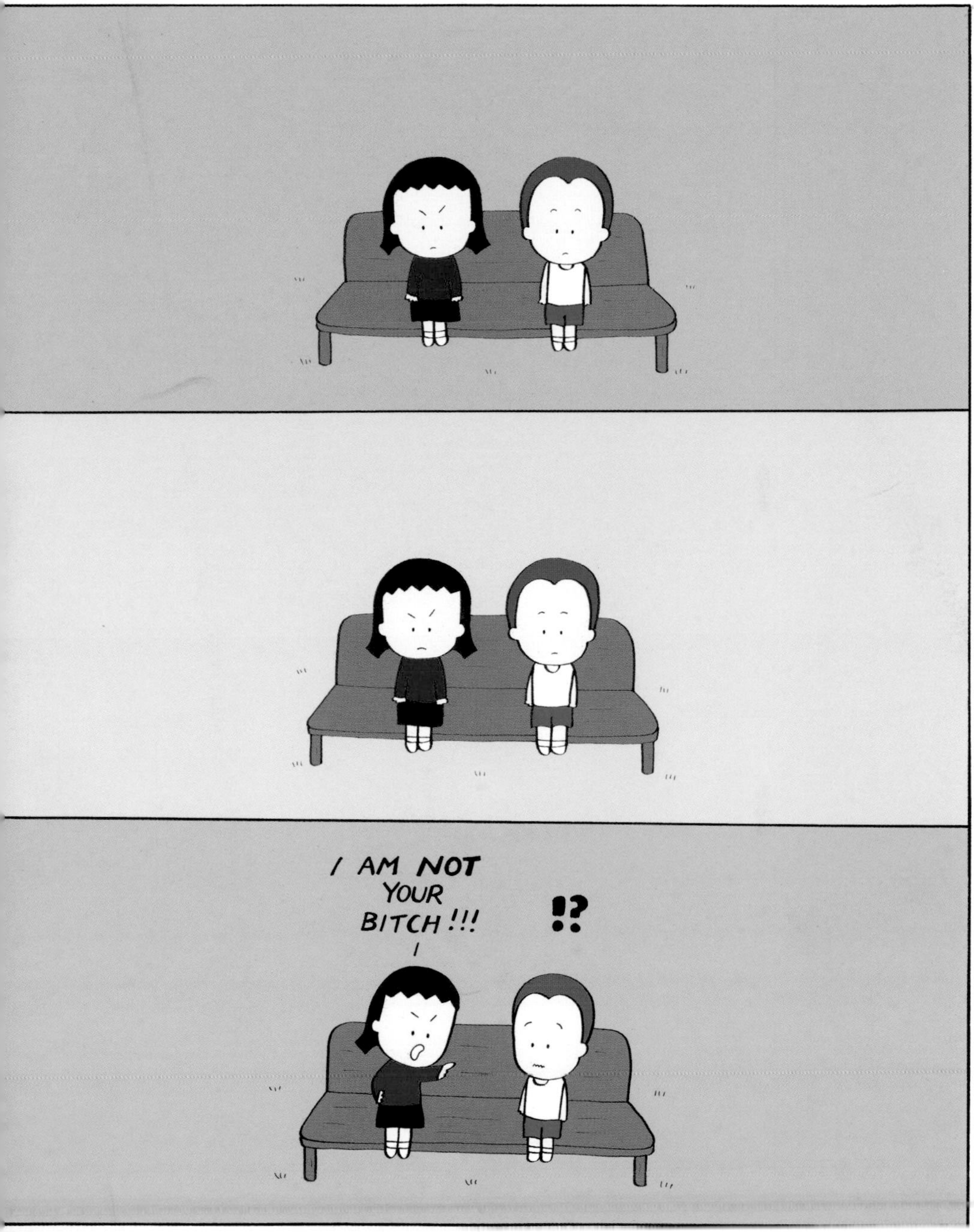
I AM NOT YOUR BITCH!!!
!?

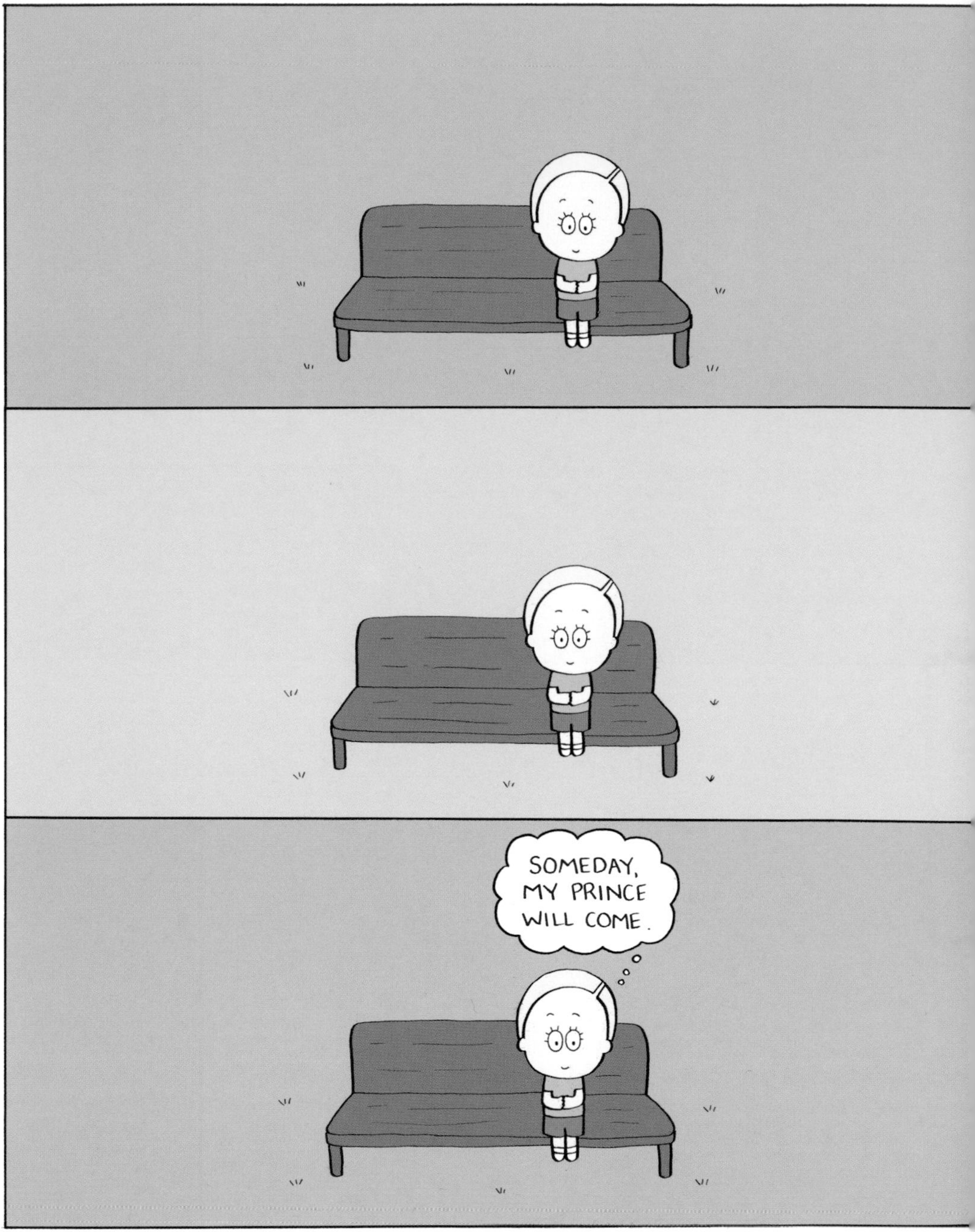
SOMEDAY, MY PRINCE WILL COME.

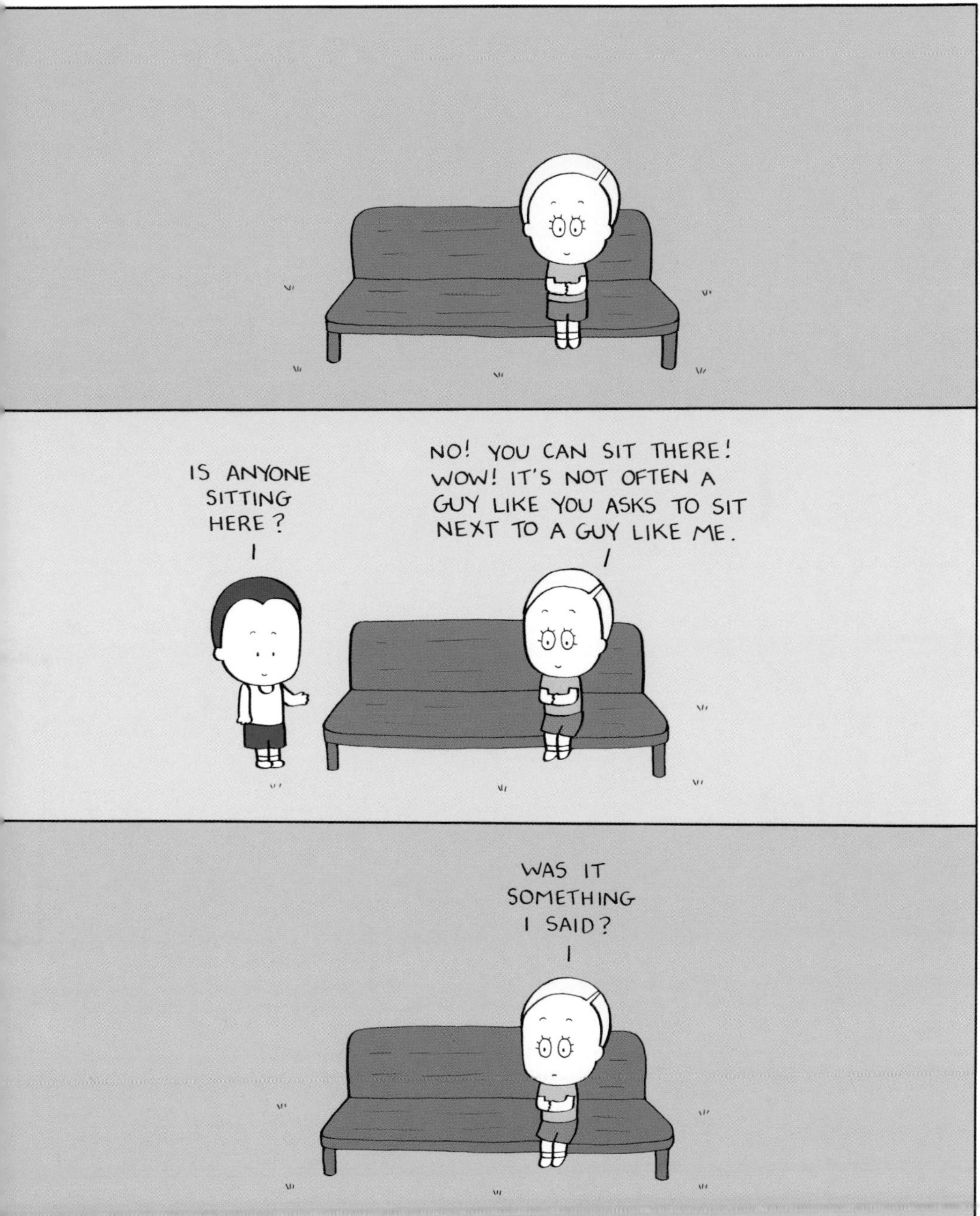
IS ANYONE SITTING HERE?
NO! YOU CAN SIT THERE! WOW! IT'S NOT OFTEN A GUY LIKE YOU ASKS TO SIT NEXT TO A GUY LIKE ME.
WAS IT SOMETHING I SAID?

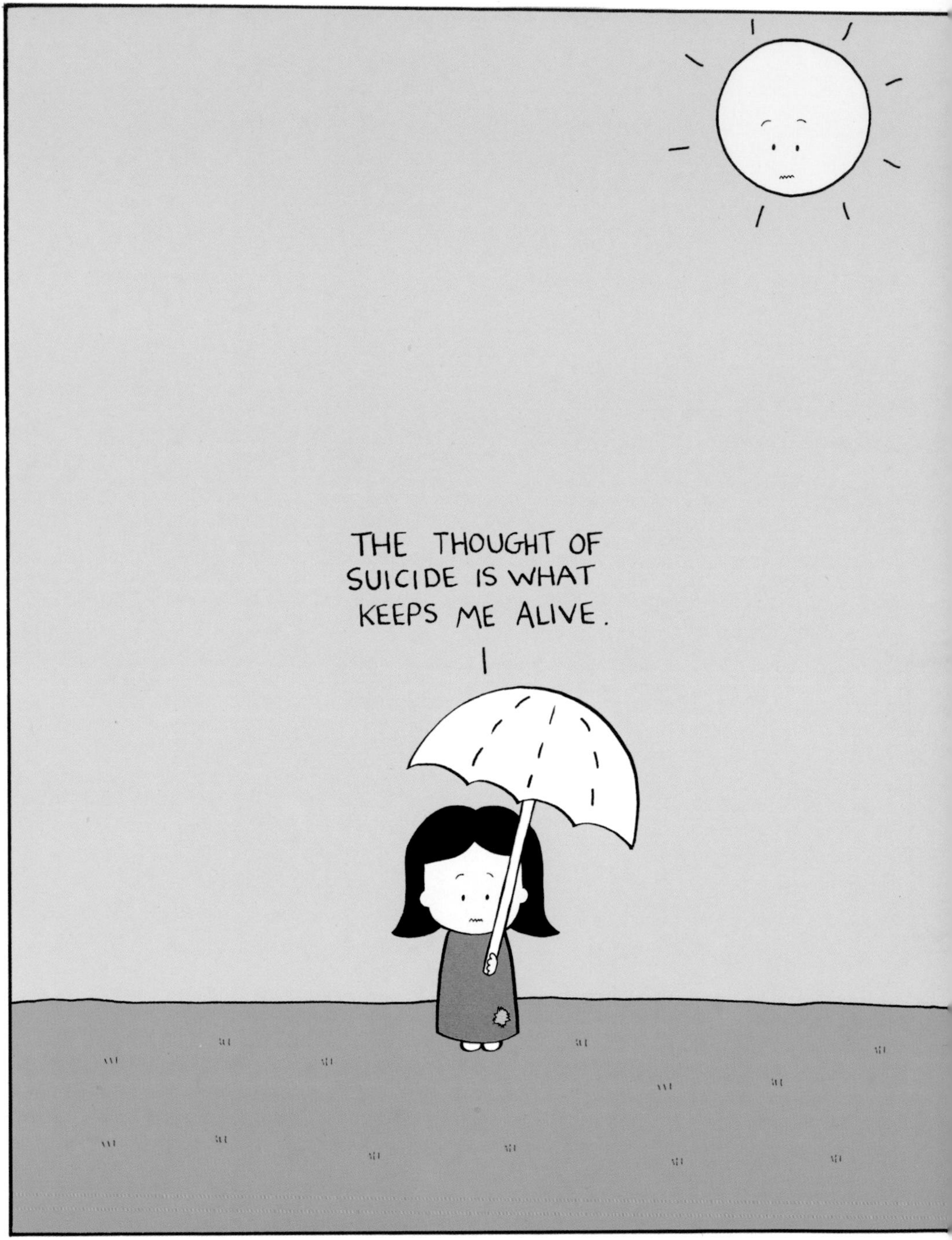
THE THOUGHT OF SUICIDE IS WHAT KEEPS ME ALIVE.

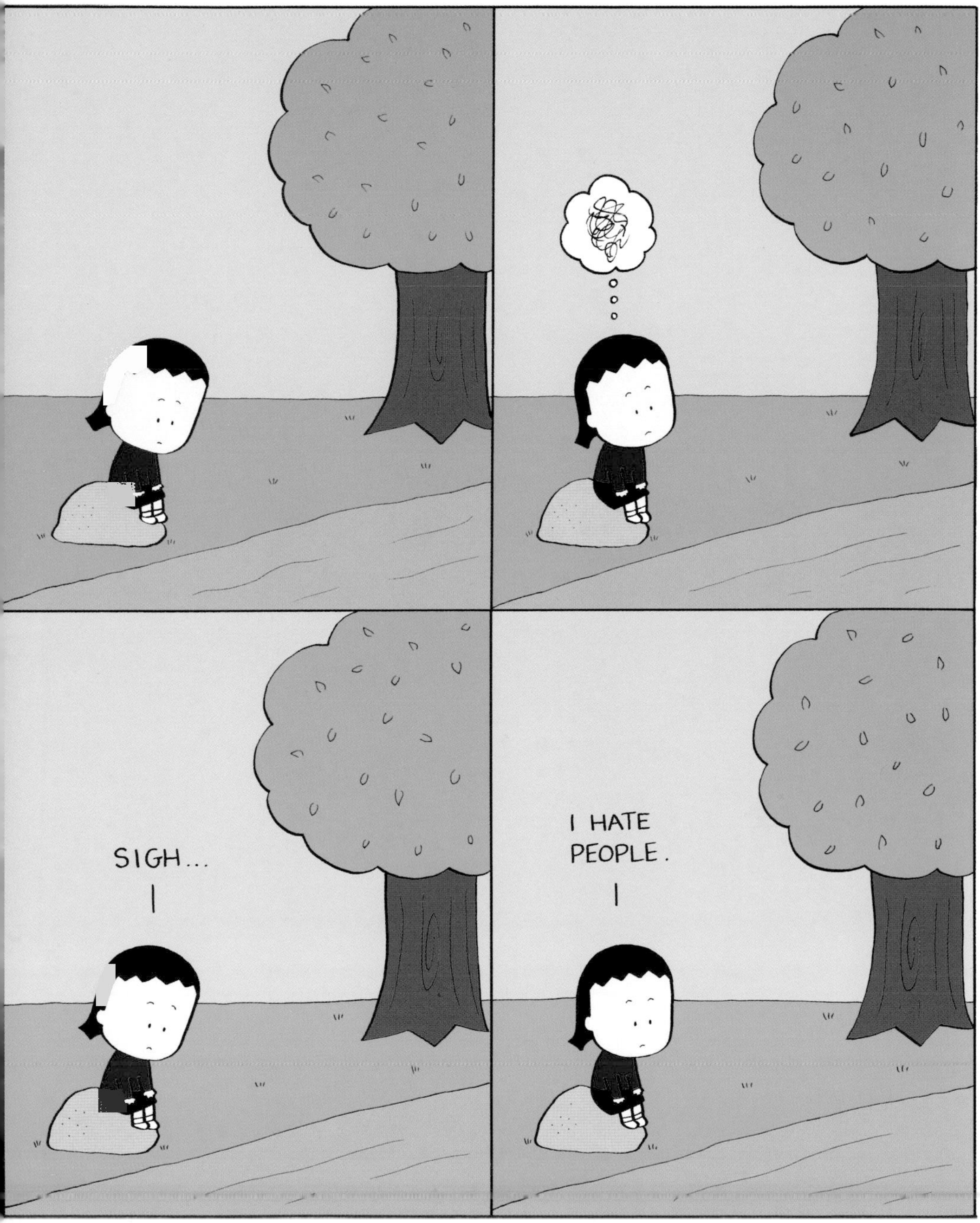
SIGH...
I HATE PEOPLE.

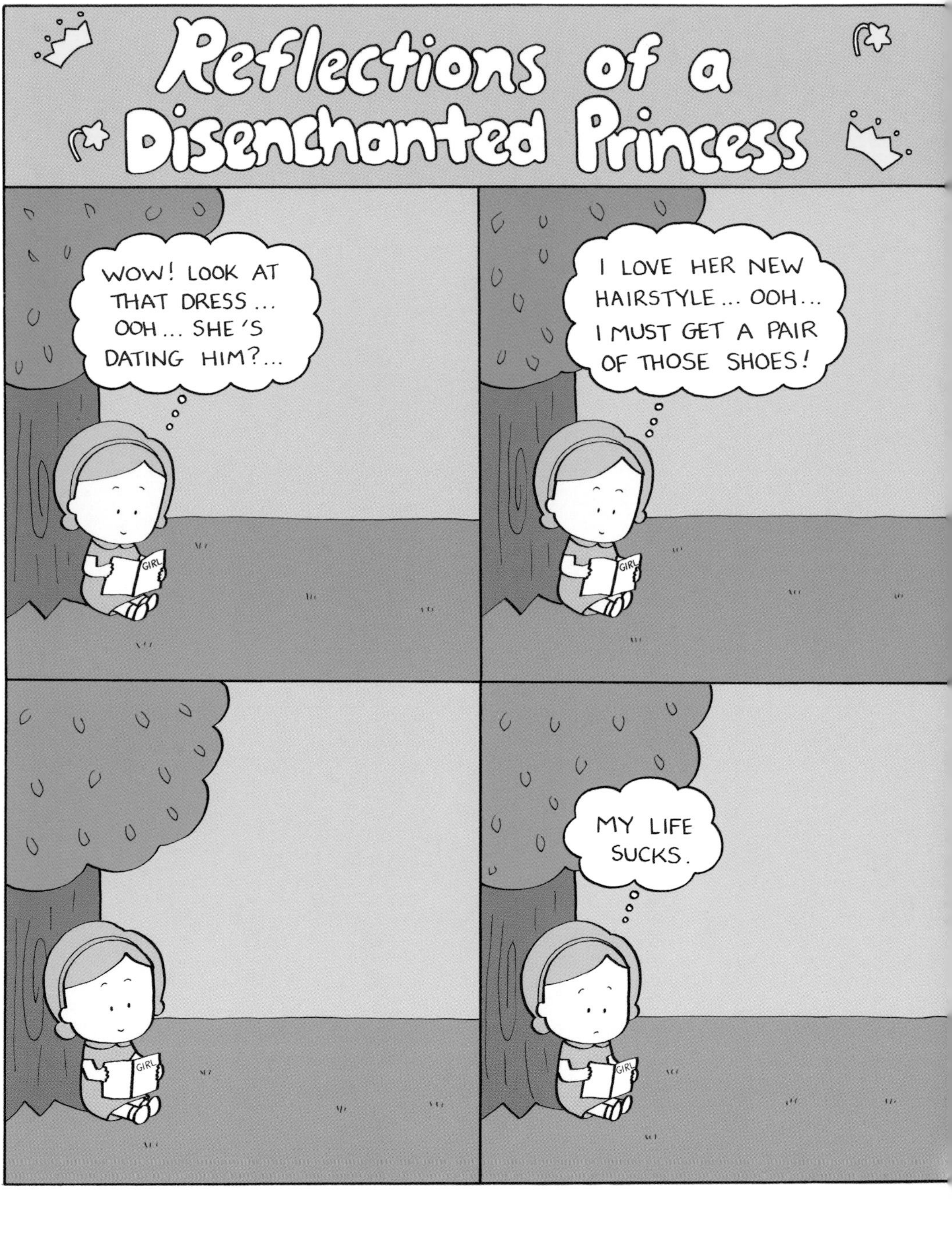
Reflections of a Disenchanted Princess
WOW! LOOK AT THAT DRESS... OOH... SHE'S DATING HIM?...
GIRL
I LOVE HER NEW HAIRSTYLE... OOH... I MUST GET A PAIR OF THOSE SHOES!
GIRL
GIRL
MY LIFE SUCKS.
GIRL

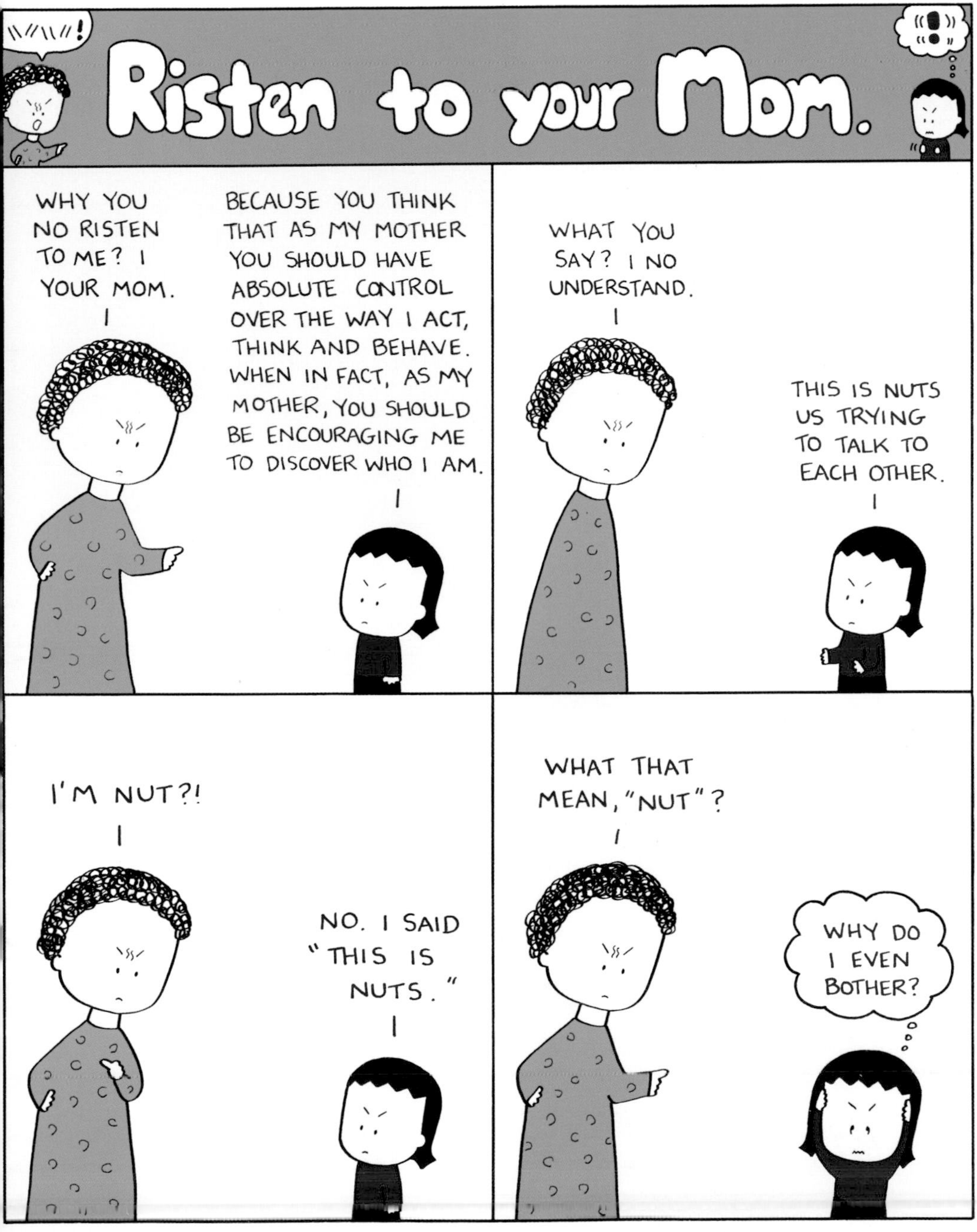

\\//\\//!
Risten to your Mom.
WHY YOU NO RISTEN TO ME? I YOUR MOM.
BECAUSE YOU THINK THAT AS MY MOTHER YOU SHOULD HAVE ABSOLUTE CONTROL OVER THE WAY I ACT, THINK AND BEHAVE. WHEN IN FACT, AS MY MOTHER, YOU SHOULD BE ENCOURAGING ME TO DISCOVER WHO I AM.
WHAT YOU SAY? I NO UNDERSTAND.
THIS IS NUTS US TRYING TO TALK TO EACH OTHER.
I'M NUT?!
NO. I SAID "THIS IS NUTS."
WHAT THAT MEAN, "NUT"?
WHY DO I EVEN BOTHER?

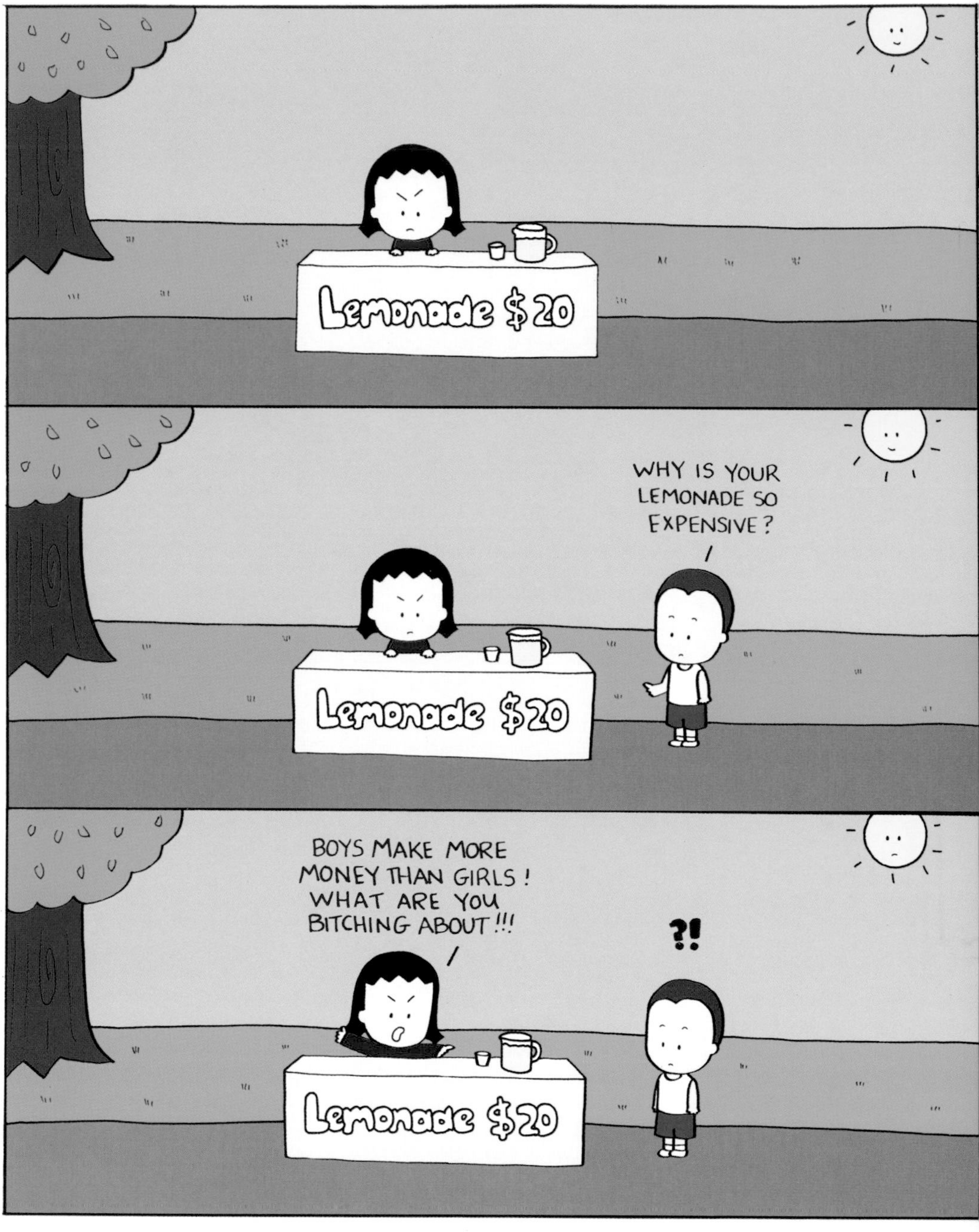
Lemonade $20
Lemonade $20
WHY IS YOUR LEMONADE SO EXPENSIVE?
Lemonade $20
BOYS MAKE MORE MONEY THAN GIRLS! WHAT ARE YOU BITCHING ABOUT!!!
?!

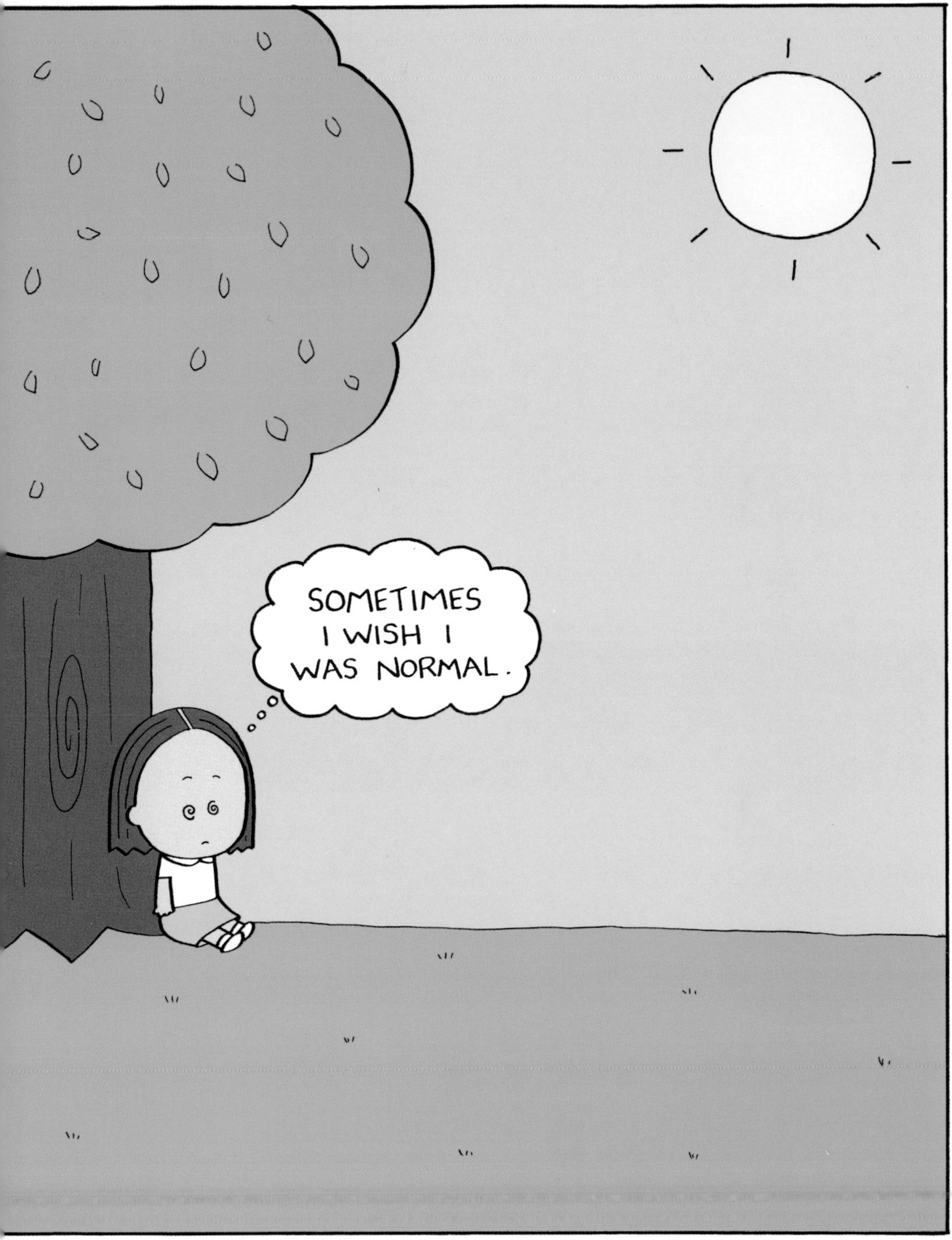
SOMETIMES I WISH I WAS NORMAL.

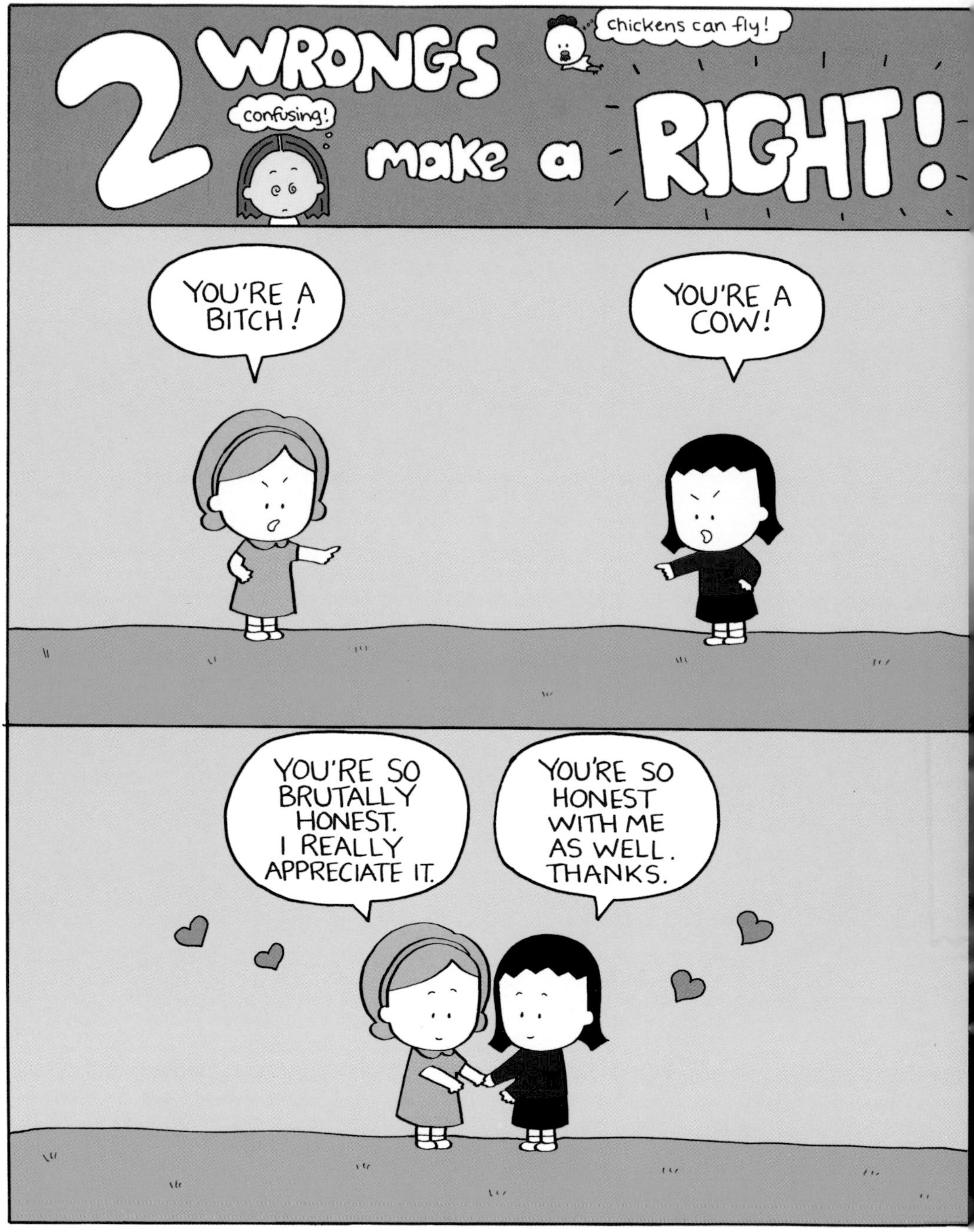
2 WRONGS make a RIGHT!
chickens can fly!
confusing!
YOU'RE A BITCH!
YOU'RE A COW!
YOU'RE SO BRUTALLY HONEST. I REALLY APPRECIATE IT.
YOU'RE SO HONEST WITH ME AS WELL. THANKS.

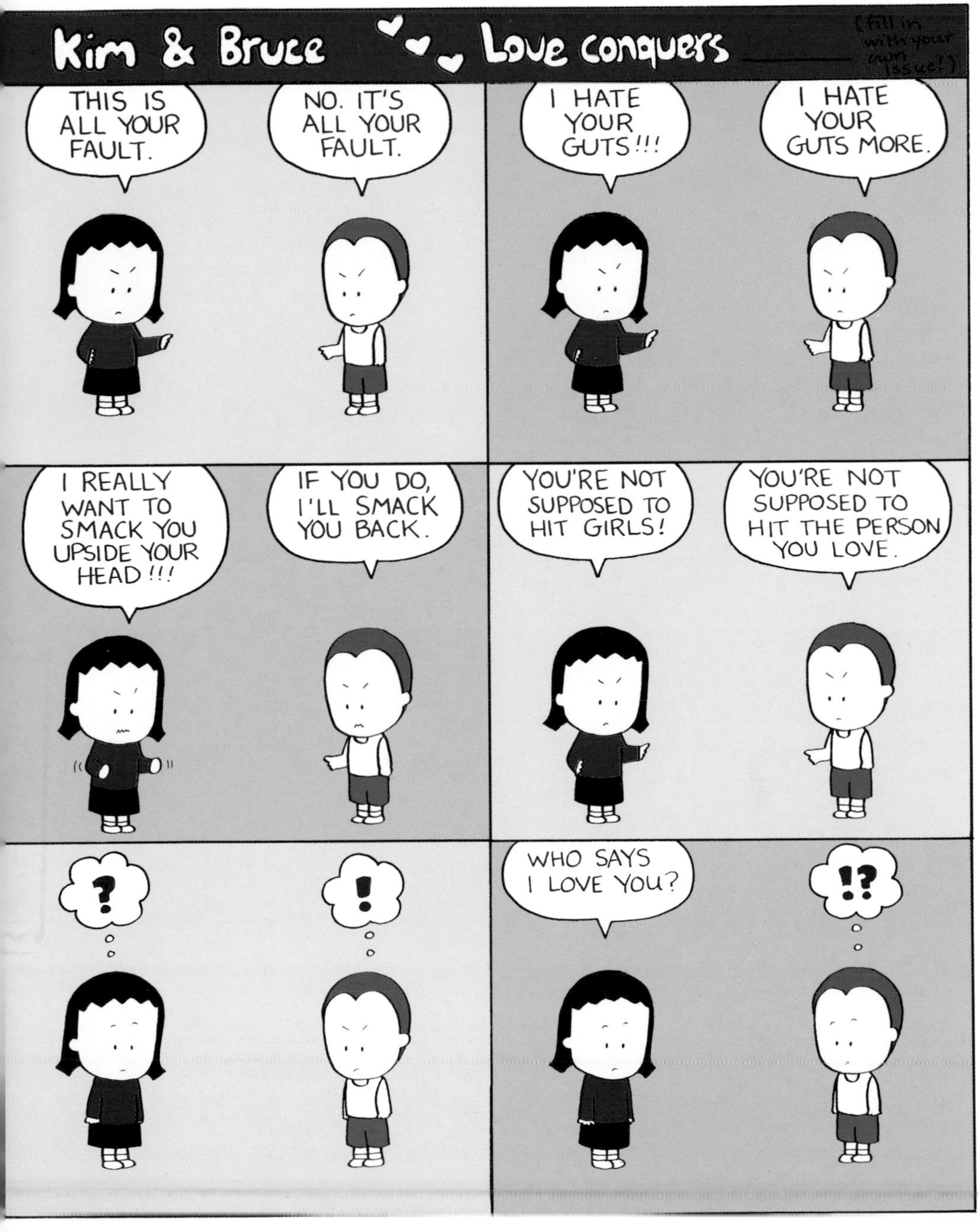
Kim & Bruce
Love conquers ______ (fill in with your own issue!)
THIS IS ALL YOUR FAULT.
NO. IT'S ALL YOUR FAULT.
I HATE YOUR GUTS!!!
I HATE YOUR GUTS MORE.
I REALLY WANT TO SMACK YOU UPSIDE YOUR HEAD!!!
IF YOU DO, I'LL SMACK YOU BACK.
YOU'RE NOT SUPPOSED TO HIT GIRLS!
YOU'RE NOT SUPPOSED TO HIT THE PERSON YOU LOVE.
?
!
WHO SAYS I LOVE YOU?
!?

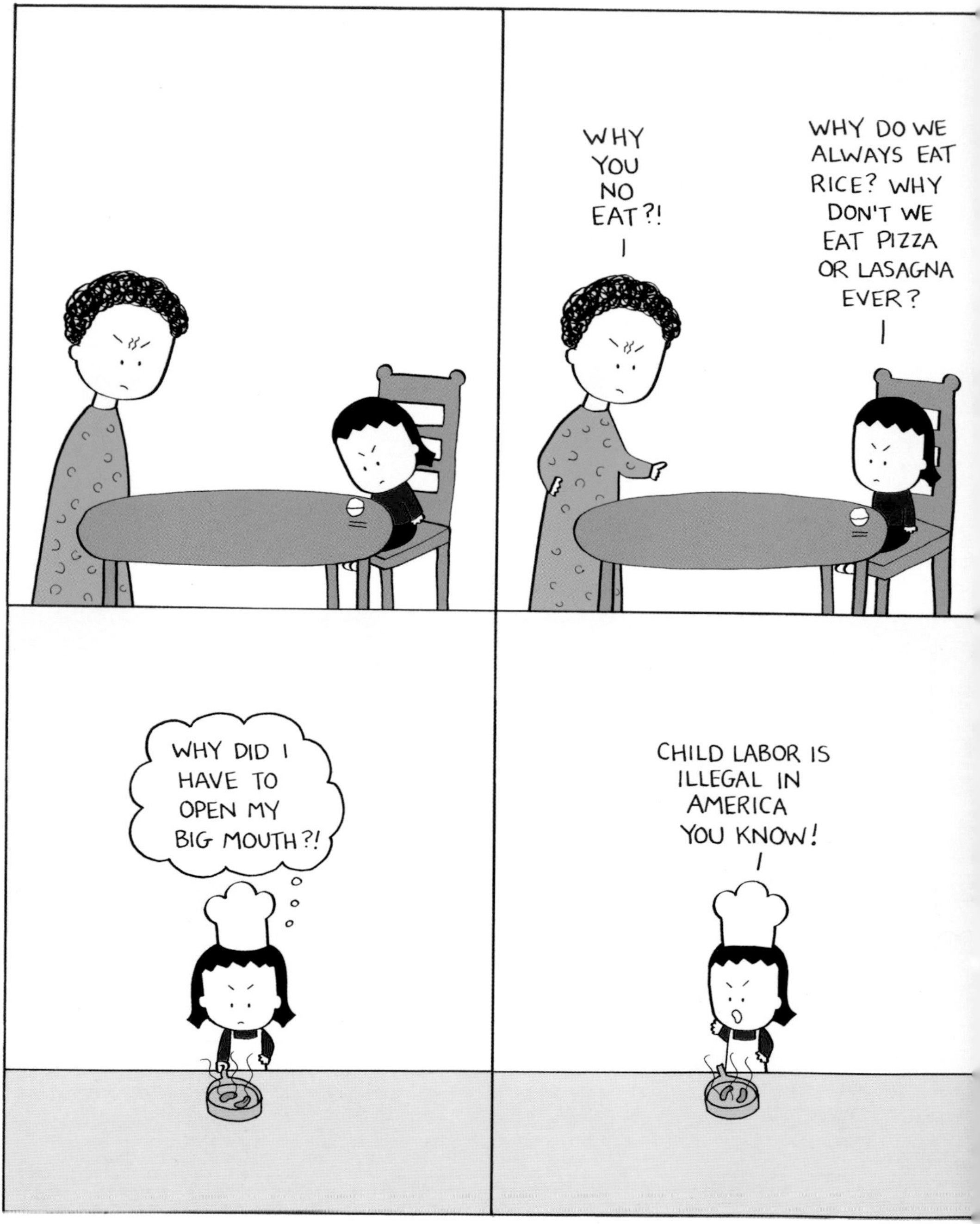
WHY YOU NO EAT?!
WHY DO WE ALWAYS EAT RICE? WHY DON'T WE EAT PIZZA OR LASAGNA EVER?
WHY DID I HAVE TO OPEN MY BIG MOUTH?!
CHILD LABOR IS ILLEGAL IN AMERICA YOU KNOW!

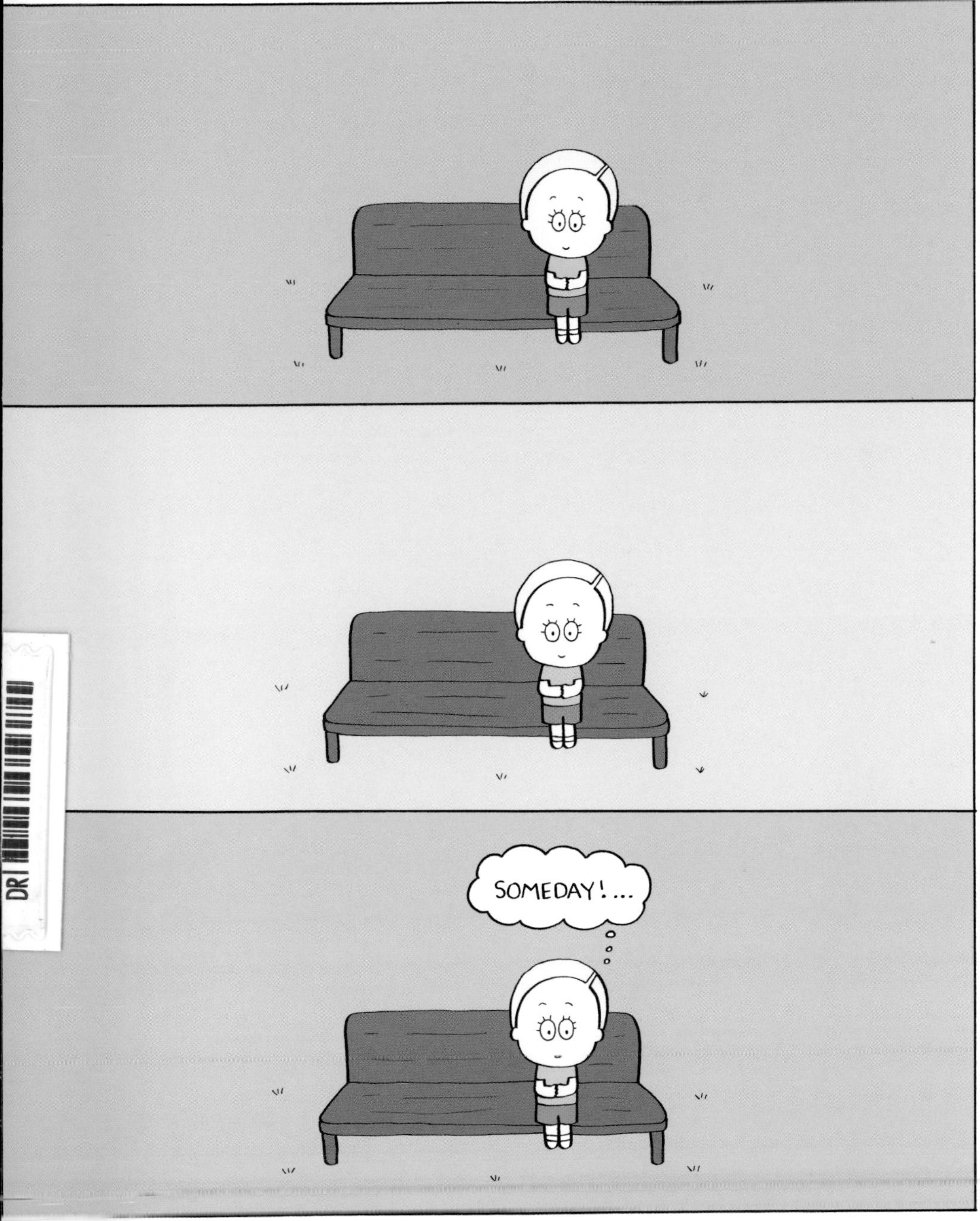
SOMEDAY! ...

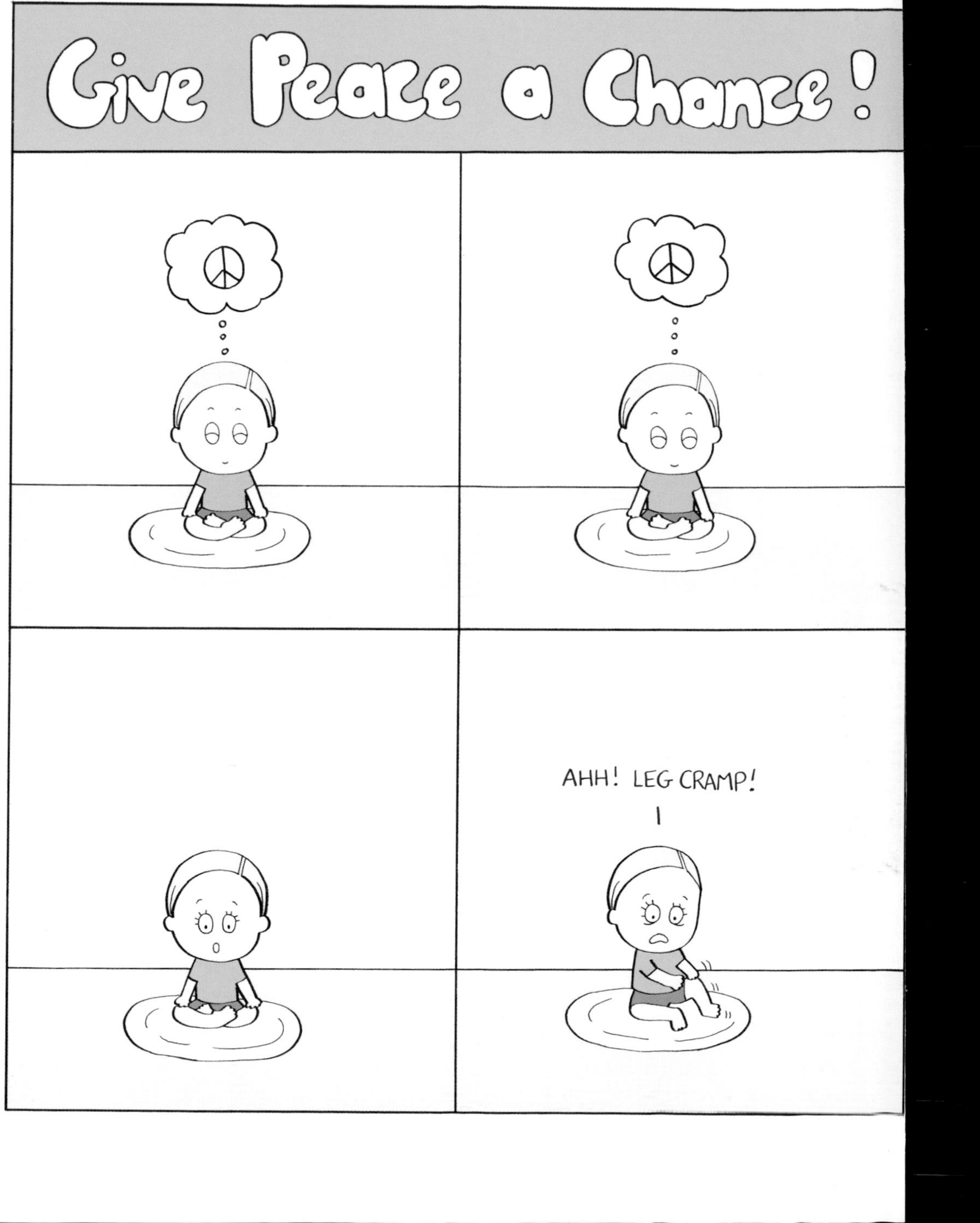
Give Peace a Chance!
AHH! LEG CRAMP!

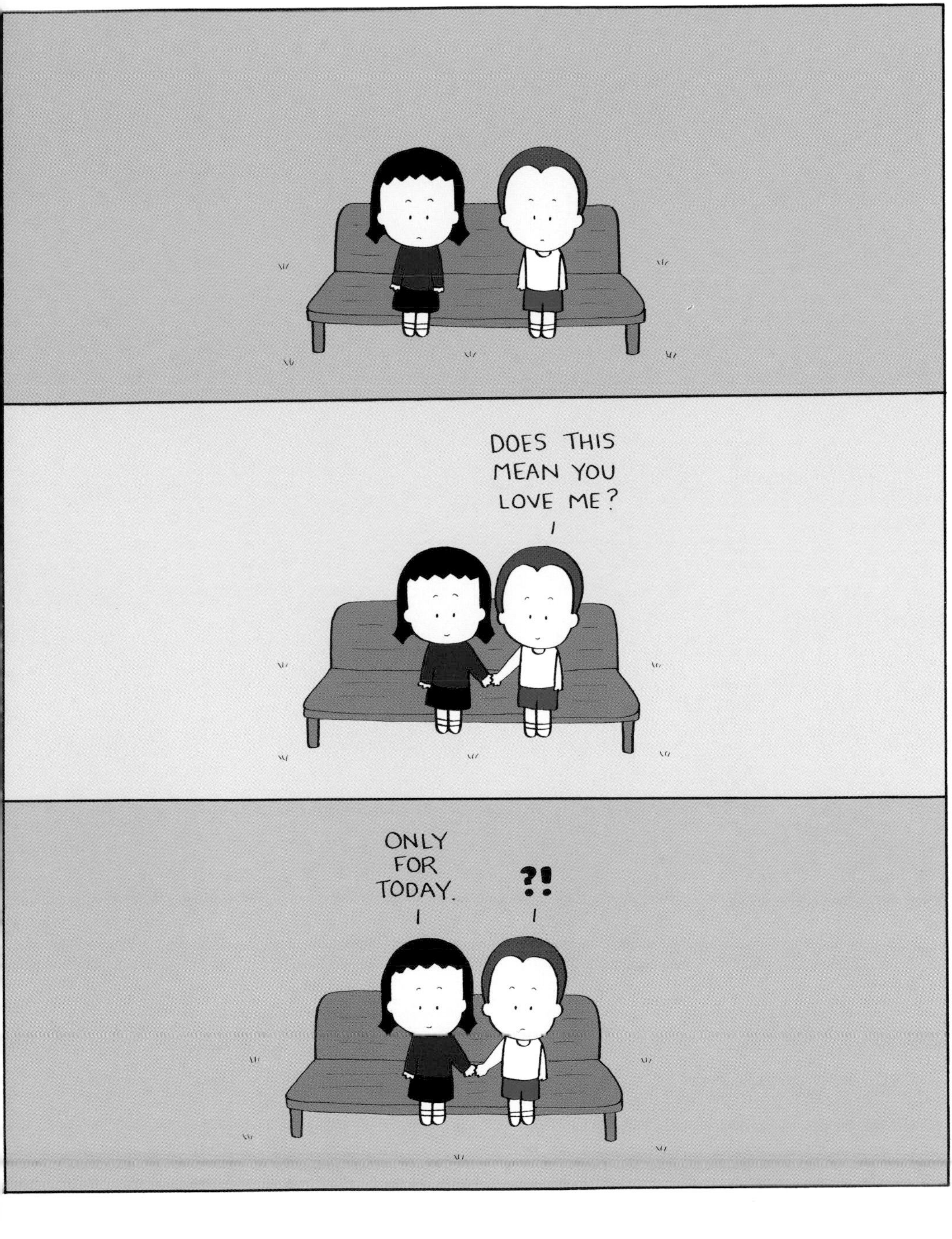
DOES THIS MEAN YOU LOVE ME?
ONLY FOR TODAY.
?!

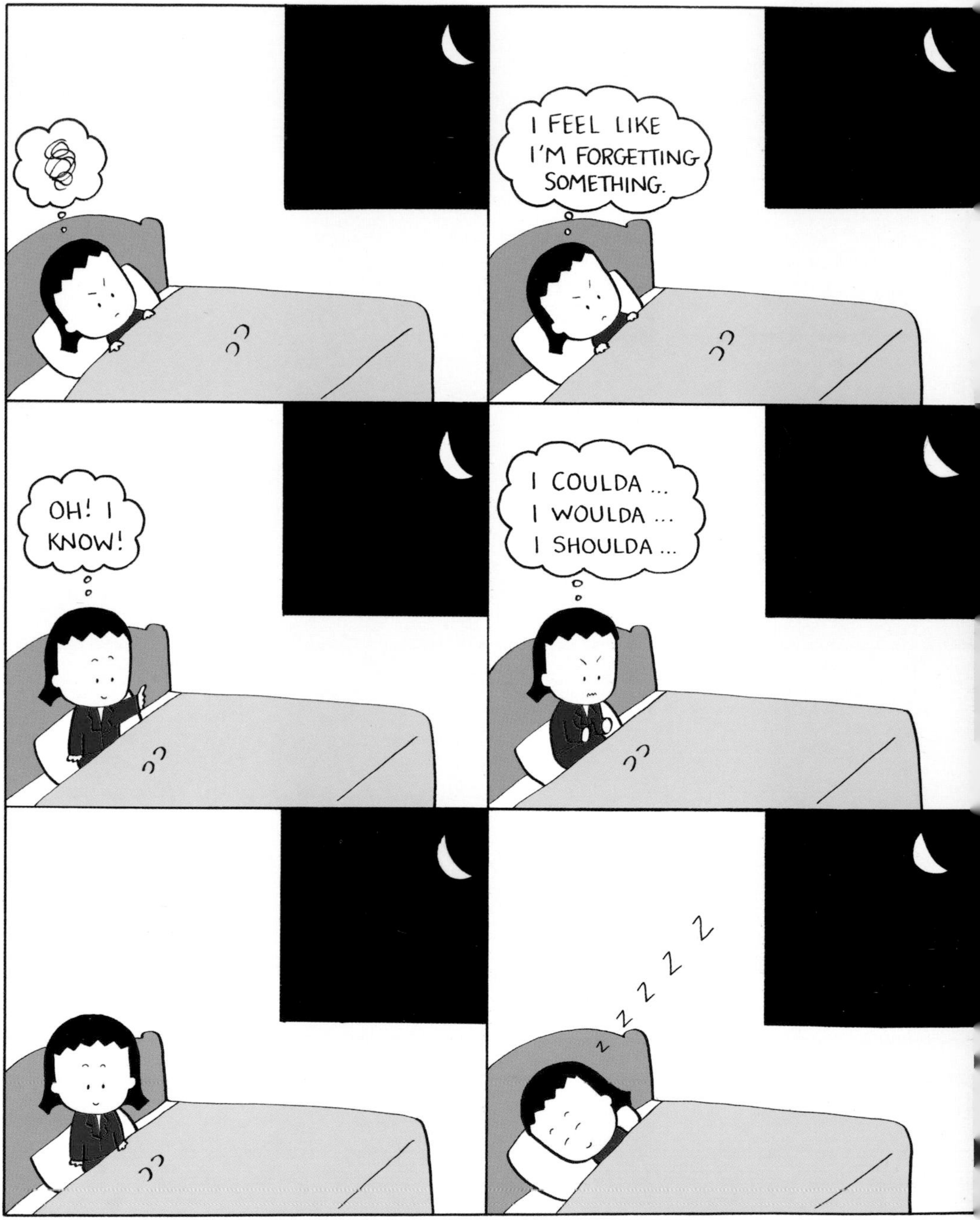
I FEEL LIKE I'M FORGETTING SOMETHING.
OH! I KNOW!
I COULDA ...
I WOULDA ...
I SHOULDA ...
Z Z Z Z Z

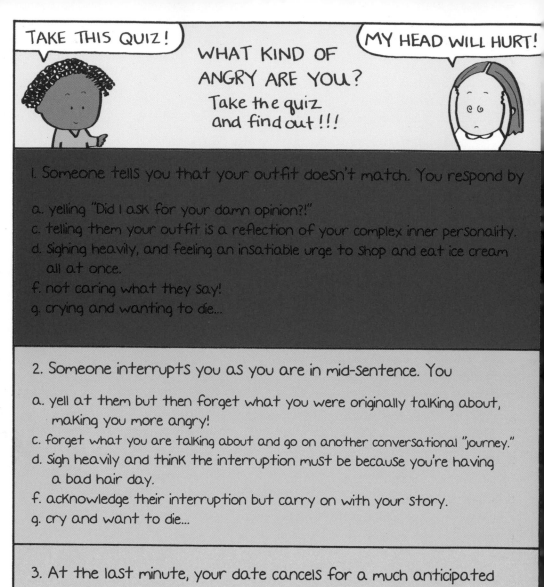

TAKE THIS QUIZ!

MY HEAD WILL HURT!

WHAT KIND OF
ANGRY ARE YOU?
Take the quiz
and find out !!!

1. Someone tells you that your outfit doesn't match. You respond by

a. yelling "Did I ask for your damn opinion?!"
c. telling them your outfit is a reflection of your complex inner personality.
d. sighing heavily, and feeling an insatiable urge to shop and eat ice cream all at once.
f. not caring what they say!
g. crying and wanting to die...

2. Someone interrupts you as you are in mid-sentence. You

a. yell at them but then forget what you were originally talking about, making you more angry!
c. forget what you are talking about and go on another conversational "journey."
d. sigh heavily and think the interruption must be because you're having a bad hair day.
f. acknowledge their interruption but carry on with your story.
g. cry and want to die...

3. At the last minute, your date cancels for a much anticipated social event. You

a. scream at them and don't speak to them for 2 weeks as punishment.
c. take your pet chicken in your date's place.
d. sigh heavily, stay home and eat ice cream all night.
f. go anyway and have a fabulous time!
g. cry and want to die...